Being Agile
In a Waterfall World

Being Agile In a Waterfall World

A practical guide for complex organizations

Joseph Flahiff

With a Forward by Jeffrey Liker

Seattle Washington
2014

ISBN: 978-1499772043

ISBN-10: 1499772041

Dedication

To my father-in-law, Richard Baker, who passed away just two weeks before publishing. Dick was always a voraciously curious scientist and I believe he would have enjoyed reading this work. He probably would have tied it back to microbiology somehow.

I know you are at peace, Dick, studying heavenly things and learning for the rest of eternity. I love you and will miss you.

Contents

Contents

Forward

By Jeffery Liker, Author of <u>The Toyota Way</u>

It seems the world has been influenced by social movements since the beginning of humanity, or at least as soon as we began socializing with each other. Social movements are generally defined as the informal coming together of people in support of a social goal, but I believe they also occur in formal structures like manufacturing corporations and hospitals and governments. We sometimes call them management trends, but social movement seems to me to be as good a term as any. A movement at the least needs a name.

The quality movement of the 1980s, when I first became an Assistant Professor at the University of Michigan, was quite energetic and visible. The initiators were the best Japanese manufacturing companies, those that were export oriented in areas like semiconductors, electronics, and auto. They were playing a different game than their global counterparts in the West. The West was playing the game of growth in volume, alongside cost reduction to boost short-term profits. These Japanese companies were playing the game of obsessively focusing on developing products that were easy to use, met customer needs, and worked. The products not only worked when you took them out of the box, but kept working way beyond any reasonable expectations at the time.

There were quality gurus like Deming, Juran, and Ishikawa who were the spiritual leaders of these movements. At that time, for most people engaged in this movement, Toyota was just one of the pack, one more Japanese company obsessed with quality. For auto competitors to Toyota they were far from just one more Japanese company, but were the toughest competitor and the one to worry the most about. In the 1980s all the Detroit automakers decided Toyota was the company to benchmark and learn from. The Toyota Production System (TPS) gained fame as a special system that was set apart from what other Japanese companies were doing. It was a total system including just-in-time, building in quality, engaging employees in improvement, and maintaining equipment that ran after decades better than much of the new equipment being purchased. Toyota was becoming "The

Machine that Changed the World," in the words of a book which coined the term "lean production."

There was a perception that this system that Toyota had evolved was bigger than quality programs, incorporating more elements that contributed to its combination of quality, cost competitiveness, and adaptiveness to the environment. On the latter, TPS became famous in Japan when the 1973 oil embargo caused fuel prices to skyrocket and pushed economies into recession. Toyota seemed to be the lone ship in the night that came out fast and strong. They later explained much of their ability to adapt was because of TPS, which included small amounts of inventory in the pipeline and the ability to rapidly changeover to the fuel efficient vehicles that were in big demand.

The moniker "lean" caught on as the name of the management movement to learn from Toyota. It was not a term used by Toyota, but it stuck. In the 1980s, Bob Cole, a student of Japanese management and a leading figure in the quality movement, said at one of our University of Michigan conferences that lean would never become a broad movement to the same degree as quality. He said it was too narrowly focused on manufacturing efficiency. He was obviously proven wrong over the decades since the lean movement is still spreading and going strong.

Of course during the decades that the lean movement evolved, there were many other performance improvement movements — theory of constraints, business process engineering, six sigma, agile manufacturing, and agile software development. They all have names and followers and people with different interpretations of what these movements mean in practice.

The starting point for Joseph Flahiff's book is the agile movement in information technology. He decides to start with a pure definition one can find in a dictionary. If you look up synonyms for agile, there are a broad range including: physically or mentally nimble, fleet, rapid, and vigorous. Certainly in an era of breakneck change that humanity has never before experienced these are good things to be. Toyota was trying to be all of these things. They knew in the 1950s that to compete with the Goliath mass producers in America they had to be the nimble and clever David that found niches and could respond quickly to changes in the market. They could not afford the high cost of mass production with all of its inventory. They could not afford the expensive single-purpose equipment. They could not afford scrap. They had neither the money nor space for all of this waste. They needed to be agile, but they were called lean in *The Machine that Changed the World*.

What makes an organization agile...and perhaps lean in the sense of eliminating waste? Toyota's answer was later defined in the *Toyota Way 2001* with two pillars of a house — respect for people and continuous improvement. There you have it. People are right at the center of Toyota's decades of success in adapting to the hyper-competition of the automobile industry. They needed people who were able to adapt to change, but with a specific purpose in mind. That purpose was always to contribute to society - one customer at a time. Accomplishing the purpose is like hitting a constantly moving target being swayed by any number of variables: higher customer expectations, new technologies, environmental impact demands, natural disasters, political activism, and sensationalist journalism. The challenges never stop, and the enterprise as a whole—from manufacturing to engineering to purchasing to IT to public relations—must be on their toes constantly monitoring the environment and adapting.

Joseph takes a somewhat critical look at the agile movement, just as I have criticized the lean movement. It is easy to turn a beautiful creative endeavor like continuous improvement into a lifeless management program to checkboxes. Yes, we have color-coded cards on the wall—check. Yes, we have organized projects around scrums with a scrum master—check. Therefore, we must be agile. Yet, look just below the surface and we see programmers spending most of their time in isolation writing code for features that customers do not understand or care about. We see beautifully written subroutines that do not play well with others written by different programmers. We see poor coordination that leads to late shipments of software full of bugs.

As Joseph makes clear in this book, the essence is still in the people and how they conduct their daily work. He asks "What if you are in a large corporation filled with silos and bureaucrats?" Bureaucracy in the form of rules and standard procedures is not bad, and in fact is the basis for stabilizing processes and organizational learning, if used properly in an enabling way. The implication of "bureaucrats" to most people are those who rigidly adhere to rules without considering whether or not they are effective. He calls for new ways of working collaboratively with managers acting as leaders and teachers, and provides ideas for what it takes to truly transform to become agile.

xvi

If you want a cookbook on decorating your walls to make it look like you are lean and agile, this book is not for you. If you want to understand the underlying philosophy and the hard work it takes to become an agile organization that can stay at the forefront of your industry, then please read on.

Jeffrey K. Liker

Professor, University of Michigan

Author of *The Toyota Way*

Acknowledgements

Writing a book is much more complicated than I had ever imagined. The number of people involved is amazing. First and foremost I want to thank my God for the kindness and grace shown to me every day I breathe. Your Spirit gives me life and all that I am is because of you. Thank you. I want to thank my wife, Jeanne Flahiff, for her love, support and indulgence throughout the creation of this book. Thank you for reading, re-reading, editing, discussing it with me, and most of all for your constant support and encouragement. You are ever my better half, thank you and I Love You!   To my daughters, JoHanna, Jillian and Joy, thank you for putting up with the papers all over the house and the constant discussions. Thank you for your support and your use of lean thinking in our home. You are an inspiration to me. To Daniel Flahiff my brother, for his hard work on the cover. To Julie Woge, my editor, thank you for being ruthless in your edits and making me look good. To the dozens of people who have read drafts and manuscripts, thank you for your input, for your challenges, and for not letting me settle for less than the best.

Why this book?

> *"The world has never had a good definition of the word liberty, and the American people, just now, are much in want of one. We all declare for liberty; but in using the same **word** we do not all mean the same **thing**."*
>
> ~ **Abraham Lincoln**

The United States was in the middle of a civil war when President Lincoln penned those words. Both sides believed they were the ones fighting for liberty. Words are important, and how we use them can make the difference between clear or confusing communications. The focus of this book is the word Agile. How is it defined, how is it used, and what does it mean.

We hear about *agility* everywhere, from *Forbes* to *Wired* and from the bluest of the blue chips to the bootstrapping startup in your neighbor's garage. In these times, as in Lincoln's, the message still rings true: "…in using the same *word* we do not all mean the same *thing.*"

The premise of this book is that *every business, every organization, every leader needs to understand the shifts that have already happened and are happening in business today.*

We are no longer living in the Industrial Revolution. We are part of the knowledge work revolution, and that revolution requires *people* who are engaged and thinking, not just a pair of hired-*hands.*

In this book I argue that any leader can begin the journey for their organization toward agility, even if the entire organization is operating in a traditional, sequential, waterfall approach to delivery of new products and services. I assert that the move from command and control management to servant leadership and trusting people is tantamount to the shift from the fields to the factories in the Industrial Revolution. I stress that the most important thing you can do as a leader to move your organization forward is to encourage your people to apply the underlying values, principles and purposes of what has become known as agile.

There is a best case scenario for becoming agile: The small to medium size entrepreneurial organization composed of teams who have worked in a startup mode to build the organization. In this organization, there are no silos. The leaders already believe in team member autonomy and the servant leadership model. The organization needs nothing but tweaking to make them run like a well-oiled agile machine.

But what if you are not part of that best case scenario? What if you are in a large corporation with silos and bureaucrats? What if you work in a government agency, or in pharmaceuticals or other regulated industries? What if you have nothing to do with software development? What if you are in marketing, or sales, or consulting? Is there any hope for you to become agile?

YES! There is hope. This book is for you.

In this book you will find the first steps toward being agile.

It is time to let go of the myth of agility as being the silver bullet that will solve all of your problems, make you effective and efficient, stop wars, and solve world hunger. It is time to get clear about what we mean when we say *agile*. It is time to develop teams, leaders, and

> What if you are in a large corporation filled with silos and bureaucrats? What if you are in pharmaceuticals or other regulated industries? Is there any hope for you to become agile?
>
> YES! There is hope. This book is for you.

cultures that are actively thinking, engaged, and continuously improving the organization.

How Transformation Happens

There are two sides to becoming agile. One side you may be familiar with is the changes to your *hard* systems. There are changes in technical practices and business processes; some are obvious and some are subtle but they are things that typically can be taught and adopted. These are the surface changes. There is another side, the people side, or the *soft* side. The people side is more subtle, but without it there is no long term change. If you just make the hard changes, they will not stick. I have seen it many times. A group starts out excited and energized about a new way of working, but they fail to change the culture and leadership. Over time these organizations slip back because they are not supported by the proper underpinnings of leadership and culture.

This book will get you started, but don't stop here. People often believe that if they can take a class, read a book or watch a video, then they will be able to _____. Fill in the blank with whatever life change you want: lose weight, stop smoking, save money, or reduce stress. Current research in brain science has proven that our brains are capable of change, even late in life. Scientists call this brain attribute neuroplasticity. [1] [2].

Neuroplasticity means that we can learn new ways of acting and responding even late in life. However, just because we can does not mean that it is easy. When we learn a new way of thinking, it takes time to erase the old and establish a new pattern. Simply receiving information does not make it our new default, even if it logically makes sense.. There are three components in any personal or organizational transformation:

- **Knowledge**: information exchange
- **Skill**: practice and coaching
- **Motivation**: the desire and motivation to change

These components are not steps or phases. They are looping and intertwined. We are introduced to *knowledge* through a number of sources: books, classes or videos. We gain *skill* through training and repeated learning.

To really learn knowledge and gain skill, we must become active learners. In my practice, I combine knowledge and skill acquisition using the Gradual Release of Responsibility (GRR), an active learning model developed by Fischer and Frye. [3]. This is not a linear model, but recursive. The sections in the triangle diagram loop around and around.

I teach *in-situ* using the GRR model. When I'm teaching a team how to do a retrospective, I schedule a retrospective that is twice as long as a typical retrospective session. I then facilitate the retrospective (*I do it*) using the additional time to interleave training vignettes. A little training, a little modeling, training, modeling.

Then, I schedule another retrospective. Before this next retrospective, I meet with the prospective retrospective

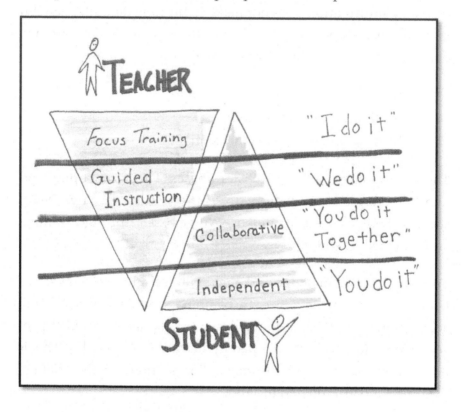

facilitators, answer questions, and walk them through the prep work. This retrospective is facilitated by me and the prospective facilitators. We work together to facilitate it (*We do it*). Depending on the situation, I may loop back to the modeling/training stage if more instruction is needed. If the team facilitating is doing really well, I step back and allow the facilitators to move forward (*You do it together*). In this case, I provide feedback after the retrospective to allow them to learn about the session they just facilitated and adapt their approach for next time. This is a critical and often missed step in the process. By co-facilitating as a team, they are practicing a model for self-supporting leadership that can happen once I am gone.

Lastly, one of the team members facilitates individually (*You do it*), flying solo for their first time. Of course, I am there, as are their peers who are learning. If necessary, we loop back to one of the other stages. I find Fischer and Frye's approach successful for many reasons. The GRR's recursive nature reinforces the learning pathways and solidifies the new learnings. It also shifts the responsibility for learning from the trainer to the learner, which allows and encourages continued growth after the initial engagement.

In contrast, I see people go to a multi-day training class and then try to implement their new *knowledge* without the *skills* necessary to be successful. When they fail, they think that it was because they cannot be agile in their context. In reality it was just that they had not learned completely. They were jumping to the end without really being trained. Skills are developed through focused effort and recursive practice.

Of our three components necessary for organizational change, we've covered *knowledge* and *skill*. Now, let's talk about *motivation*. Only when we have motivation will we actually start to see change. John Kotter's first step in his well-known eight step change process is: *Step 1: establish a sense of urgency*. [4]. Without motivation there will be no change, all we have is knowledge and skill. Someone can want to stop smoking or lose weight. They can know how and understand the process completely, but without motivation it is just not going to happen. Developing a sense of urgency is important in your efforts to change. This may come from the fear of an imminent failure or the desire to seize an opportunity, or any number of other ways.

This book is one element in your journey. A great starting place for you to gain knowledge and begin the journey. It will show you *how to start becoming agile in any organization.*

What is in this book?

In Chapter 1, I help bring clarity to our discussions by exploring the way people use the word *agile.* I assert that, although commonly used as a noun, agile is not a noun; it is an adjective. Using it as a noun has caused, and continues to cause, not only confusion but dismay. You will learn the four things people really mean when they say the word *agile.*

Chapter 2 explores the changes in the way we think that are necessary when we move from a predictive way of thinking to an exploratory, agile, way of thinking. You will learn how being agile is not just a different way of delivering products and services; it is a different way of conceiving of our work.

In Chapter 3 we explore how your organizational structure impacts agility. We will examine why organizations with projects, portfolios, and PMOs *always* struggle with agility. You will also better understand what you can do if you are in an organization where you have these organizational structures. Yes, you can still be agile.

Chapter 4 will expand your understanding of what it means to be agile. I introduce you to the concepts of agility horizons, nested and variable agility. These concepts will help you see that being agile has nothing to do with software development. Any business can benefit from agility.

In Chapter 5 I introduce the four aspects of agility: technical practices, business processes, organizational culture, and leadership approach. We will discuss how the balance of these four aspects will help you in becoming and staying agile in your specific context.

Chapter 6 introduces five core practices that anyone can implement in any business context. If I was working for a waterfall based organization, these are the first five things I would implement. These five things generally do not require you to get anyone's permission to begin, yet they will have profound impact on your project and your team. They could be the starting point for becoming agile in your organization.

There are some important topics which need addressing but did not fit well within the flow of this book. These are found in the appendices. The first appendix discusses the Agile Manifesto for Software Development - what it is and what it isn't, and what is important about it. The second appendix explores a number of myths and misconceptions associated with agile and clarifies these items for better understanding.

Any leader can build agility in their organization. It takes a radical focus on the importance of people and creating a culture that engages the mind and supports creative thinking. I encourage you to read this book and question everything in it. Get a study group together and discuss it. Create a community of learners who will band together and try it. When something is difficult and seems as though it is not working, dig deep into *why*. Maybe what is stopping it from working is just what you need to focus on changing. If you find a better approach to something, contact me I would love to hear about it.

In the first chapter we begin by looking at two projects that exemplify the kinds of results you can see when the pieces come together.

Why be agile?

Why would an organization want to become agile? What is the benefit?

Introduction

> *Ring. Ring.*
>
> *"Hello, Uh huh. Ok. Really. Ok. I understand. Yes, I will let the team know… Thanks. Goodbye."*

The year was 2009. The Clarity Initiative[1] was the CEO's personal pet project and one that he passionately believed would change the healthcare industry for the better. With a three year budget of over $8.5 million, the project included a team of 100 brilliant actuaries, designers, testers and developers. A previous similar project ended up costing the company a lot of money and a lawsuit. Because of this history, fear and internal politics had kept

---

[1] Name changed for privacy.

it from delivering several years prior. Some people within the company believed that if we went forward with the project it would actually destroy our market leverage and be the literal end of the company. The project stalled for a year in attempts to deliver in a traditional sequential (waterfall) way. They just couldn't get past the fear of another lawsuit.

The organization decided to take a different approach. Rather than trying to get all of the requirements right the first time, we looked at the whole initiative and selected the most important work to begin delivering first. We delivered in little increments and allowed those internal people who were afraid of the project to see exactly what we were doing before we launched anything. With each little increment, they made some adjustments. This kept everyone happy enough to not block the initiative.

We were a year and a half into the project with four releases behind us and another year and a half to go, when I received a phone call. With that call it was all over. The project was cancelled. Mid-flight. On the bright side, while nearly the entire organization was using the waterfall (sequential) delivery model, we had chosen to take an agile approach, and once again it had paid off. The first payoff was breaking down the political barriers. The second payoff was that we had prioritized our work and delivered the most valuable features first. Everything we had in the pipeline at the time went live immediately and added value right away. Yes, it was sad. Yes, we all wished it would keep going, but we had delivered what the customers needed. And we had not lost a year and a half of work.

Nine months later I received an email from one of the business leads on the project. He was excited to tell me that the site we built won a major national award for providing customer value! How many traditional projects cancelled in the middle can say that they would have a similar legacy - awards, pride of workmanship, and most important of all, customers using and getting value from the system! It was a huge win for the company, the team and the consumer.

Now that's what I call agile.

A few years later, I left that organization and formed Whitewater Projects, Inc. to help other companies and organizations adopt an approach to delivery that would allow them to see these kinds of results. It is exciting to see groups succeed. But what makes me even happier is hearing how it changes cultures and changes lives, bringing hope and joy into their work.

While working with the Washington State Department of Licensing to help them become agile, they were using the Scrum approach to deliver a website called *License eXpress*. The team had just completed a pre-release demo to the support team who would service people using the system...

"That is great. The system looks good... But what is going on here?" the customer service agent inquired.

"Huh? Sorry, what do you mean?" the developer answered.

"I have never seen anyone from IT at this point in a project (just before launch) so happy…what's going on?"

The developer, with no small amount of relief, proceeded to tell them about their agile approach. The *License eXpress* system had been working for months. Every two weeks they would add a couple more fully tested and complete features to the system. This gave them the confidence in the quality and stability of the deliverable, unlike their past projects where testing always got cut short at the end of the project. Under the old system, there was always a question as to whether the system would work when it finally went live. This time, however, there was no fear when it was time for the system to go live.

That story always makes me smile! Those people had hope and joy in their work. Their fear, like that of the Clarity project team, had been removed because they had seen the system long before it went live.

These stories illustrate two key concepts:

- Quick, iterative, and incremental delivery of value
- Shift from a mind-set of needing to control the work like a mass production system to enabling creative knowledge work

These are some core ideas that support agility, which you will learn more about in the following chapters.

Agile vs. Waterfall?

It is likely that you have seen blog posts with some variation on the title "Agile vs. Waterfall" more times than you care to recall. It has bothered me for years. At first I didn't know why, but deep in my gut it bugged me. Initially it was for the simple reason that I don't think they are necessarily mutually exclusive. I also don't believe one is better than the other for all cases. There are times when it makes sense to be agile and there are times when it makes sense to use a sequential approach.

Back in the 90s when agile was just beginning, there was a real rebellion against the use of the traditional, sequential, waterfall approach to project delivery. This approach had been used well in construction, but when applied to knowledge work it was falling miserably short. A new agile approach was developed. It was more applicable to knowledge work.

Now the pendulum has come full swing and what we see in these "Agile vs. Waterfall" blog posts is the same story from the 90s, just with the players reversed. The argument promoted is that agile should be used for everything. Isn't this the same problem in reverse?

There are places where agile makes perfect sense, and there are places where a more planned upfront approach makes more sense. There has to be a balance. But to achieve that balance, we have to first understand the two approaches and clear up some confusion. So let's start with defining the word *agile* more precisely.

Multiple Meanings

Listen to people when they talk and you will find when they use the word *agile*, they really mean one of four things or maybe all four at the same time. This can make clear communication difficult because one person is thinking of one definition and another is thinking of a completely different definition. The four most common meanings that people have in mind when they say agile are:

- Being Nimble

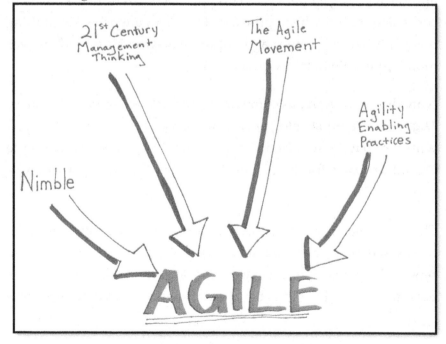

- The Agile Movement
- 21st Century Management
- Agility Enabling Practices

In the next several sections, we will explore these concepts.

Nimble

We hear about agile all the time, but what is it really? Does it apply to your work? Isn't it just a software thing? Agile in the Information Technology world has really become the "in" thing.

Let's look at the dictionary definition of agile:

> **Ag-ile** (ăj'ə l, -īl'): adj.
>
> *1. Characterized by quickness, lightness, and ease of movement; nimble.*
>
> *2. Mentally quick or alert: an agile mind. [5]*

Did you notice that little *"adj."* after the phonetic spelling? You may already know this, but that means it is an adjective. An adjective is a part of speech used to describe something. Examples include:

- Happy
- Sad
- Slimy
- Round

- Fast
- Slow

- Orange
- Soft

Any word that describes the attributes of a noun is an adjective. It is not possible to DO an adjective. Try to DO orange. Or, try to DO happy. You cannot. You can only do things that make you happy, or that make you orange (spray tan?). They are not things you can DO.

However, as often happens in the English language, the word agile when used in the software development context has morphed from an adjective to a noun in many people's minds. A noun is a person, place or a thing. A noun is something that can be or that is. It has existence. Changing a word that describes a noun to a noun is significant and the cause of much confusion.

Many words have experienced a similar change. When you want to look something up on the Internet, we "Google it." Google used to be a proper noun: the formal name of a business, Google, Inc. We all know that a Kleenex is what you use to wipe your nose. Kleenex is actually a brand name, but it has become the industry term for all tissues. In a similar but unfortunate twist, agile has been "nouned." It has stopped being an adjective - a word used to describe aspects of a person, place or thing. People talk about "using agile" and "implementing agile," or the "agile methodology." The reason this is unfortunate is that, as it has happened, it

> Throughout this book we will use the term agile in this way, as synonym for *"Nimble"*.

has changed what the word agile means in these contexts. People in our business have lost the intrinsic meaning of the word as a descriptor.

The really confusing part is that it has become a noun for people who are in the software development business. It has not become a noun for people in the rest of the world. In business for example, when a CEO of a company says they want their company to be agile they mean they want it to be nimble. They do not mean that they want to implement an agile approach to delivery.

Agile isn't a thing to be implemented or used. It is not a methodology or framework. It is an adjective. As an adjective, it describes the nature of a thing. But in common practice, agile has become a noun, particularly in the software industry. It has come to mean implementing a set of practices, principles, or frameworks such as Scrum or XP. While implementing Scrum or XP will often times result in the organization becoming agile, just using XP or Scrum does not by definition make you agile. Only when you exhibit the attributes of agility - being nimble, quick, with ease of movement - can you justifiably call your organization agile. Throughout this book we will use the term agile in this way, as a synonym for *nimble.*

The ability of a business to be nimble has become increasingly necessary for organizations in the 21st Century. The global economy has become a place where change happens so quickly that the businesses that will survive are those which are most nimble. They are in the best position to capitalize upon the changes in market demand, technology innovation, and emerging production/distribution models.

Business Agility

There seems to be quite a bit of confusion about the use of the word agile between business and software people.   When I read magazines or blogs such as:

- Business Week
- Harvard Business Review
- Forbes
- Fortune
- CIO
- SearchCIO.com

In these sources the term agile is frequently used but it is not used to reference a methodology, it is used as the pure adjective that it is, meaning nimble. However, when my friends in the agile community use the term, they do not typically use the word in the same way. They typically use it to mean a set of prescribed business processes and thinking that, when used together tend to create organizations that are nimble. It is a much narrower use of the word and I think it limits options and stifles creative thinking.

If agile is defined as nimble, then let's refine our definition to make it more applicable to the specifics of doing business and running organizations. Here is how I define the business term *agile*:

> **Ag-ile** (ăj'əl, -īl'): adj.

> **1. The ability to adapt appropriately, as fast as, or faster than changes occur in the business context.**

Let's peel that onion a bit. First, let's look at *"the ability to adapt appropriately."*

Ability means you have the resources, the means, the skills and the know-how to do something.

To adapt is to make something so that it works or makes sense in a new use or a new purpose or intent. If I adapt my presentation style to match my audience, I will change it depending upon the group with whom I am speaking. If I am speaking with CEOs, I will use different language than if I am speaking to a group of developers.

Appropriately is an adverb. It modifies the word "adapt." To be appropriate is to be suitable for a particular purpose or occasion. To adapt appropriately is to make something to work in a new context that is suitable for that context.

Next, let's look at *as fast as or faster than changes occur…* This seems to imply speed, but that isn't necessarily the goal. If changes occur slowly, then "as fast as or faster than" isn't necessarily speedy. It means *at the same or faster pace.*

If you adapt appropriately but at a slower pace than the industry around you is changing, then you will get left behind (Zone 3 below). If you adapt appropriately as fast as, then you are keeping pace, which might be OK as long as no one else is keeping pace

(Zone 2). The third place to be is in front, adapting appropriately faster than the industry is changing (Zone 1).

If you have ever watched surfing, then the illustration below makes sense. Sitting behind the wave, you will not move because

there is no force. Sitting on top of the wave, you are riding it. This is a safe place so long as you are pushing the front of the cresting wave. But the place where the most energy can be found is right in front of the wave. There the energy is propelling you forward.

Some organizations want to be in Zone 1 and some want to be in Zone 2. That all depends on your business model. No one wants to be in Zone 3. Those businesses are just in the process of becoming obsolete.

21st Century Management

In the early part of the 20th Century, the Industrial Revolution changed the face of business though the centralization of manufacture and the drive for economies of scale to help reduce costs and maximize the productivity of the workforce. The organizations that could process most consistently and lock down the distribution channel for their products were the most stable and unchanging. They survived and thrived.

When the Industrial Revolution began, people all over the world were moving from being farmers and craftsmen to working in factories. In the factories, workers were trained in one task that they were expected to repeat over and over with ever increasing precision and *efficiency*, enabling *mass production*.

In the first 14 years of the 21st Century another shift has occurred, the shift from mass production to knowledge work. Knowledge work is any work that requires you to think. The most important product then is the minds and creative ability of the people on our teams.

When some people use the word agile they mean to say 21st Century management - practices and thinking that support knowledge work and innovation. The management methods also tend to improve the working context of all workers in any industry, even in mass production. There is nothing inherently agile about 21st Century management thinking, although it is often associated with agile or with the agile movement, sometimes it is even called *agile thinking*, but it does not specifically facilitate agility.

In his book <u>Drive: The Surprising Truth About What Motivates Us</u>, Daniel Pink identifies three 21st Century business practices: autonomy, mastery and purpose. Pink describes autonomy as the ability to be self-directed rather than controlled. His and other research has shown that people become more engaged and do better, faster, more creative work when they are able to set their own direction. We will discuss this in greater detail in chapter eight. Mastery is the idea that people get excited about getting good at something. That is why we learn to play music in our spare time. We get excited when we conquer a new skill. Pink identifies *purpose* as the third driving factor in what motivates people in the modern economy. When people connect with a purpose, they fully engage their complete creative selves. This is why people are willing to spend hours of their free time contributing to things like open source software and WikiPedia.

Carol Dweck presents another 21st Century management concept, which is the idea of having a *growth mindset* . A growth mindset is the belief that abilities, skills and talents are not fixed but may be changed and improved with work. This is in opposition to a person with a fixed mindset who believes that those traits are fixed and unchangeable. These are examples of the kinds of 21st Century business practices that are important to have in all areas of business, not just in development areas.

The Agile Movement

The Agile Movement is what has happened in the software delivery industry since about the late 1980s and early 1990s. At the time, object oriented (OO) software development was one of the key turning points in software development. OO made it possible to more simply conceptualize and create very complex systems and to modify them.

"The Agile movement is not anti-methodology, in fact, many of us want to restore credibility to the word methodology. We want to restore a balance. We embrace modeling, but not in order to file some diagram in a dusty corporate repository. We embrace documentation, but not hundreds of pages of never-maintained and rarely-used tomes. We plan, but recognize the limits of planning in a turbulent environment." — Jim Highsmith, History: The Agile Manifesto [6]

Between 1995 and 2001 the Internet grew dramatically. At that time software projects were still generally thought to be like any other project. Thus when projects got large people felt the need to manage them in order to make sure that money was not being wasted. The common construction management approach of sequentially (waterfall) executing the work was used to manage software development. A small but growing community of people began to take a different approach. They drew inspiration from many and varied sources including: Lean Manufacturing; trends in product development such as what is described in the *Harvard Business Review* article, "The New, New Product Development

Game"; the Theory of Constraints (TOC);, Spiral Development; and many others.

In February of 2001, a group of 17 software development consultants gathered together in Snowbird, Utah at what was billed as, "The Lightweight Methods Workshop." They came to talk about what they were finding as they were trying to develop software with lighter weight management and more flexible planning than traditional methods. The result of this conference was the creation of the Agile Manifesto for Software Development. This is one of the key milestones of the agile movement.

See the appendix for a brief history and understanding of the Agile Manifesto, including some online interviews with the authors of the manifesto

Many, if not all, of the creators of the Agile Manifesto for Software Development, were interested in Lean. This is very evident in the methods and language used in many of the agile methods. In my experience and observation agile is the software development implementation of lean.

The following Venn diagram shows the relationship I have found. Lean is a much larger topic than agile. It encompasses manufacturing, distribution, whole systems thinking as well as new product development. Although it is not talked about nearly enough, agile being a new product development approach has more in common with the Toyota Product Development System (TPDS) than it does to the Toyota Production System (TPS). Unfortunately, fewer people have been exposed to TPDS, than have been exposed to TPS.

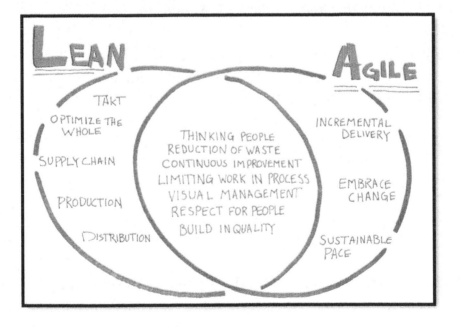

Agility Enablers

As I have said, agile used to be an adjective that described the nature of a noun. Now the meaning has become:

> *Doing some set of known practices such as: Scrum, XP, Kanban*
>
> *Or,*
>
> *doing the things in the Agile Manifesto.*

You have probably heard some agilest say, "If you are not doing _____, you aren't agile." Fill in the blank with that person's favorite agile enabling practice:

- Scrum
- Continuous Integration
- Kanban
- Kaizen
- Retrospectives
- Delivering every 2 weeks

Please hear me, these are likely all good things to do based upon the context that the person speaking is either in or has experienced. However, they are not the determining factors of your organization's agility. Practices, methodologies, and frameworks can only *enable* you to be agile. Similarly, the values and principles in the Agile Manifesto are all enablers.

This next sentence borders on heresy in some agile circles. *None of the values or principles are NECESSARY to be agile. They all enable agility.*

> *Is it possible to be agile (nimble) without holding to any of the values or principles of the Agile Manifesto?*
>
> *Yes!*
>
> *Is it likely?*
>
> *No.*

> *If you hold to the values or principles of the Agile Manifesto, will it automatically make you agile?*
>
> *No!*
>
> *Is it likely to help?*
>
> *Yes.*

The values and principles of the Agile Manifesto have been proven over time to be key enablers of agility.

If you want to improve your chances of being agile (nimble), you will want to take a long hard look at what is said in the Agile Manifesto. These values and principles make it easier and more likely that the business can respond as fast or faster than the changes that are coming at them. They enable the organization to be agile. But they are not absolutes. They are not immutable. They are just good practices. Many of them draw from a wide variety of good business and education practices and mind-sets.

Throughout the rest of this book we will explore these practices and mind-sets to extract which are explicitly agile enabling and which are more broadly, good business practices that also happen to enable agility. For example, working in iterations is an agile practice that not everyone needs or will benefit from. Organizations where the outcome is well known do not need to iterate. On the other hand, excellent teamwork will benefit any organization.

Returning to the Waterfall

Let's return to our agile vs. waterfall topic from earlier in the chapter. If the definition of *agile* is nimble then the opposite of agile is not *"waterfall"* as is often implied or even explicitly said. The opposite of agile is "heavy, slow, stiff, awkward, clumsy, lumbering, slow-moving, ponderous, ungainly, unsupple." It may be that waterfall makes you slow, heavy and stiff, but not by definition.

Given this, when we hear that organizations need agile, we will not be thinking that they need some prescribed methodology, set of tools, or framework. Rather, we will think that they are heavy, slow, stiff, slow-moving, unsupple, and that they need to be able to adapt appropriately as changes occur in the business context. This is a much more open approach to agile than a narrow definition based upon things like the Agile Manifesto (see appendix).

Chapter Summary

There are four possible meanings when you hear the term *agile* being used: Being nimble, 21st Century Management, the Agile Movement or Agility Enabling Practices.

In this book I will be very specific about which element we are discussing.

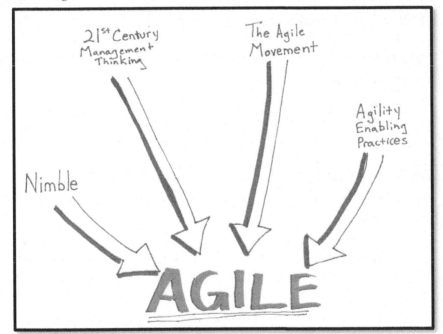

The opposite of agile is not waterfall. The opposite of agile is slow, lumbering and unadaptable. So, there is really no reason to write articles about agile vs. waterfall as they are not in conflict. Taking a nimble approach to some work is great. Taking a more planned and predictive approach to others is also great. But there is a lot that can be adapted from 21st Century Management - the agile movement and agility enabling practices can improve the quality, predictability, and culture of traditional sequential projects.

Selected Resources

The following are selected books and online resources that relate to this chapter. I recommend these resources to further your study of what it means to be agile.

Management Innovation, Changes in management in the 21st Century and where we are headed next.

> Hammel, Gary (2007) *The Future of Management*, Boston, MA: Harvard Business Review Press

Toyota New Product Development Process/Lean Product Development. This is not the same as the Toyota Production system or Lean for manufacturing.

> Ward, Allen C. (2014) *Lean Product and Process Development*, Boston, MA: Lean Enterprises Institute, Inc.

> http://www.slideshare.net/JeffLiker/morgan-liker-slideshare-v13

Business Agility (not software agility)
> http://blogs.hbr.org/2014/01/build-a-quick-and-nimble-culture/
> http://www.forbes.com/sites/stevedenning/2012/04/09/the-best-kept-management-secret-on-the-planet-agile/

Agile Software Development

http://www.agilemanifesto.org
http://www.agilealliance.org

Action Plan

Now What?

Examine how you use the word *agile*. Be clear about what you mean when talking about agile. Do you mean:

- Nimble
- The agile movement
- Agility enabling practices
- 21st Century Management Thinking

Think

You may be thinking to yourself that discussions (arguments) you have seen, heard or been part of may never had happened if you had been clear about what you mean when you say agile

Act

For at least the next week, commit to using the word *nimble*, instead of *agile* and when the world nimble does not make sense, you will use the appropriate words for what you mean.

Share

One great tool for learning is to teach someone else. When you teach you tend to pay closer attention and learn more deeply than if you were not going to teach someone else. Commit to starting a conversation with 2 or more people regarding how the word *agile* is used in your organization.

Mental shifts

Being agile isn't just a different way of delivering work, it is a whole new way of thinking about work.

Introduction

There is a common misconception that is deepened by the "nouning" of the word *agile*. That misconception is that agile is a methodology, a different way of delivering work. In actuality, obtaining a lasting move to agility takes a complete re-evaluation of how work is conceived.

Command and Control

During the Industrial Revolution, it was believed that the workers were generally too unsophisticated to understand the work they were performing. This belief played very nicely with Fredrick W. Taylor's interpretation of the Scientific Management approach, where leaders setup hierarchical *tall,* as opposed to flat, structures. Each lower layer is subordinate to the higher in both authority and autonomy. Decisions are made at the top of these organizations and the lower layers are expected to follow. The lower you go in the organization the less authority and autonomy the people have. The very lowest are the *hired hands,* those who just do the work and are not paid to think. This was the perspective of Fredrick W. Taylor and Henry Ford back in the early 1900s.

Improving efficiency and reducing variation are important to achieve if you are in assembly work, which dominated business in the 20th Century. In the early part of the 20th Century this was accomplished by the *command and control* approach, but over the decades approaches to management changed through theories and practice like the Toyota Production System, Lean, and the Theory of Constraints. As noted in the sidebar, Liza Woods states that the approaches have changed the face of a good part of the manufacturing management world by putting a strong focus on the people who do the work and putting authority for decision making in their hands.

There are still many organizations (in every industry) that hold onto the command and control type of approach to management when a more humane approach would actually result in more efficiency/effectiveness, and a better work environment. Why do people hold to these ideas? In some cases it is because they are necessary. But in a far greater number of cases, it is because the managers *feel safe*.

> *"Having worked in technology manufacturing, it always chafes me when I see/hear discussion that ties together manufacturing with command and control rigidity. I know it's a concept that is easy to explain to anyone, which is why it is used so often. Why it chafes me, particularly from Agilists, is that most of the Agile practices (Scrum, Lean, Kanban, Theory of Constraints, plus a lot of ideas from Deming) come from manufacturing.*
>
> *The sector that is often being used to describe command and control is in fact the one that has evolved the most in the last 40 years and influenced agility the most.*
>
> *In any uber-chaotic world, we see the same command and control behavior but it is in an effort to dampen the chaos and feel secure. For people showing this behavior, the traditional practices are more of a warm fuzzy security blanket. They feel that when they are surround by the artifacts of traditional practices that everything is going to be all right (even if it isn't)."* – Liza Wood

Command and control, even the name sounds safe. Things are under *control*. I personally practiced much of the traditional approach to project management for the better part of a decade. The problem is that there are good and bad aspects of these traditional approaches, and it is often difficult to untangle the two. There is nothing wrong with planning work in a sequential way. When you are building a bridge, you want the steel and the steelworkers to arrive at the same time, so you need this kind of upfront planning. When you are dealing with work that is well known and for which the processes are understood, planning the work is possible. But there is no need to be a dictator. Servant leadership will achieve the same results with less stress and more engagement from the team. The *command and control* approach makes the assumption that there is one or a few all-knowing leaders who give commands, much like the military. But as Captain David Marquet shows in the *online extra*, real delegation with both responsibility *and* authority create not only a more pleasant work environment but a stronger organization over all.

Online Extra

Captain David Marquet's talk on Greatness, based on his book,

Turn the Ship Around!:

http://bit.ly/distributed_decisions

During the years that I was working at the Fred Hutchinson Cancer Research Center, I was primarily doing traditional, sequential projects (waterfall). I was the project manager responsible for the IT spaces, pathways, cable/wire/fiber, networks and systems in the new buildings between 1999 and 2005. For these projects I had a team of technology architects, Registered Communications Distribution Designer (RCDD) engineers, and other experts. My approach was always that of a servant leader.

When I was working on a project, one of the first things I would do is get the team together to develop the plan for the project. There was no way I was going to try and develop it myself. The team knows better than anyone how they are going to execute the work so they should create the plan for the work. I was doing work that was truly sequential, and yet used 21st Century practices (including servant leadership and team empowerment/autonomy). Sequential projects do not need to be command and control.

Competitive Advantage

In the early days of the Industrial Revolution, competitive advantage was obtained by efficiency through economies of scale and through control of the supply/distribution chain.

In the last part of the 20th Century, the source of competitive advantage started to change. Mass production and supply/distribution chain control was disrupted by new innovations. The Internet and the rise of the personal computer changed the face of business, created industries and created a *new economy*. An economy based on knowledge work. It can be seen as a shift from the industrial mass production economy to the knowledge work economy. This shift is just as significant as the Industrial Revolution. Before the knowledge work revolution, improved efficiency and reducing variation were valued. Now, creativity, innovation and speed to market are key. The term *first mover advantage* - the idea that whoever got into the market first could dominate - became a common phrase.

Unfortunately, for many organizations, management practices did not adapt with the change. We have continued to use the same 20th Century management practices like *command and control* to manage a radically different business context. Reduction in variation and improvement of efficiency are the exact opposite of what is needed to be nimble.

Since the emphasis in growing 21st Century organizations is not upon delivering the same thing over and over, new management practices are necessary to meet the new emphasis - the ever changing customer demands. Change and variation are not things to be avoided, but things to be leveraged for strategic advantage. This is the gap that agility fills.

You know this in your gut already.

Our traditional approach to delivery, as seen in the diagram, is to place a ring around a specific scope of work and fund that work as a project. The project then goes through a fairly standard set of

sequential or nearly sequential steps, elements, or stages as seen here.

But you and I both know that isn't how it works. Half way through the project an executive gets an idea or hears from a *key customer* that something needs to be different, and the requirements change. Then the questions ensue:

Who should pay for it?

Why didn't anyone think of this before?

How will this impact our ability to go live and what will it do to the budget?

Followed by the ultimatum:

I don't care…We need to do this and still hit our dates. And, no, you don't get any more money to do this work;

it should have been in your scope to begin with.

Reality looks a little more like the following image.

Does that look familiar?

Of course it does. If you have spent any time in business, you have lived this story. But here is the real problem. No one wants to admit this is happening. The reasons for this are many, and have a lot more to do with psychology than they do with project delivery. We intrinsically like process; it makes us feel comfortable. Process is logical and apparently reasonable, so it should work. However, process doesn't exist in a vacuum. People are involved, and people are messy and quite illogical.

Our Systems Are Optimized...

Our systems are optimized to create the results we are now getting. If we want different results, we have to change the system. The *systems* I am talking about include our organizations, our cultures, our leadership, our business systems and our technical practices. That means if you have budget overruns, if you have late deliveries, if your quality is low and you get customer complaints, your systems are *finely tuned* to create those outcomes.

In the example of a sequential project that was interrupted mid-project with a change in requirements, the system is optimized to have requirements show up mid-project that derailed the project. It should not be surprising that additional requirements showed up.

The only way to stop getting those results is to do something differently. You cannot keep working with the same system and expect different results. It is the system that is creating those results. Time to reboot. Time to get radical. It is time to change the system!

All too often businesses do not have what it takes to be nimble and adjust to the changing markets. The command and control approach designed for optimizing efficiency in factory settings is intentionally rigid. This rigidity allowed for maximizing conformance and coordinating the factors that improve delivery in predictable systems, especially when attempting to move people from being farmers or crafts people to being factory workers. Unfortunately, this is just the opposite of what you need to be nimble.

Why Agility?

Pick up any business periodical or search any reputable business news site and you will find article after article about the rapid rate of change, the constant need for innovation, the need for business to be agile, nimble, flexible and adaptable. There is no contesting that being able to quickly adapt to changing conditions is necessary to today's business, but are you? Is your organization able to adapt to change? Do your technical and business practices, your culture and leadership support being nimble? If your organization has not made a specific effort to make it nimble, then the answer is most likely, no.

No company can assume they have a long term competitive advantage in anything. Whole markets exist that didn't exist before:

- Online shopping
- Crowd funding
- Cloud computing
- Big data

Markets that existed for decades are disappearing or radically changing:

- VCRs & DVDs
- Credit card industry
- Camcorders
- 35mm film

Markets change so quickly it can make your head spin. Nowhere is this more obvious than in the music industry. Here is a business that was tightly controlled and had long lead times. Musicians had one way of getting their music produced, and that was through a music label such as Sony Music Entertainment, Bertelsmann Music Group (BMG), PolyGram Records, Warner Music Group.

These companies controlled the distribution channel, they controlled the product creation, and they controlled the marketing. If you didn't have a contract with a label, you likely weren't going to make it big.

Then along came technology to disrupt that market. Napster, LimeWire, and others changed the face of music. These illegal sites freely shared music in files between computers. While they were shut down for their illegal trafficking of files, they did change the industry. Soon thereafter the iTunes store was open. The music industry shifted from selling whole albums on records or CDs to one where individual songs were chosen. You didn't need to get the whole $15 album when you could just buy a song for about $1. Spotify and Pandora offer another step in the music industry's transformational journey. With Spotify and Pandora a person can now listen to any song or whole album without buying it at all. Who knows what the next innovation will be in the music industry.

A similar revolution is taking place in book publishing. New technologies have made it easier than ever to publish a book, with or without a publisher! There are hundreds of companies that will help you self-publish your book either in hardback, paperback, eBook or audio book format. This has revolutionized the publishing industry and converted it from a highly controlled and long lead time market, to a nimble and short lead time market.

Name a market and the same thing is happening there too:

- Banking – Online banking services, PayPal, WalMart
- Insurance – Esurance, Progressive
- Retail sales – Amazon, eBay, Etsy
- International importing - Alibaba
- Travel – Expedia, Hotels.com, Orbitz, Kayak

Some businesses successfully make the switch and some do not. What is it that characterizes those that successfully make the transition to the new fast pace of knowledge work? The collapse of the American financial markets in 2008 was long in coming, but the demise of Lehman Brothers was fast and furious. I was foolish enough to be one who believed that because Lehman Brothers had been around forever, they would recover from their slump. I should invest while they are down. Well, they didn't stop going down, and I never got my money back. Things are even more severe in emerging markets where losses are more likely and can be high.

Speed in markets can bring not only loss but great opportunity. Brian Acton and Jan Koum created WhatsApp. Koum created an app that would put status by people's names in a telephone address book. Cool idea but no one really used it. That is until Apple announced push notifications. WhatsApp used push notifications allowing people to push their notice out to their friends/network. Suddenly people started to use the app. Only once people started using it did Acton and Koum realize that they had accidently created a messaging service. They shifted their focus and took advantage of what their customers were doing. WhatsApp was purchased by Facebook in 2014 for an amazing $19 BILLION, that is with a 'B'. Amazingly, WhatsApp was only five years old when it was purchased, but it had 450 million users. Acton and Koum were agile, and it gave them the competitive advantage to see an opportunity and seize it. The rest is history.

What does your business do? Is it in a market that is changing? Lehman Brothers didn't think they were. Chrysler and GM didn't think they were. Don't make the same mistake. Every industry is ripe for change in today's volatile marketplace. Organizations that explode and become the next WhatsApp are those that have their eyes open for opportunity, are designed to move quickly and nimbly. Because they are agile, these organizations are prepared to jump on it when opportunity strikes.

Vanity Publishing:

As an interesting side note, self-publishing a book was once called "Vanity publishing" because self-published books had not been through the vetting process and the publishing companies owned the distribution channel. Self-published books were not really *legitimate* published books.

When I began writing this book, I considered finding a publisher because that is just how books are done, right? Well not necessarily. I spoke with many authors and read several articles, and as with so many industries, the printing industry has changed. The distribution channel for books, especially technical books is no longer controlled by the publishers. It is controlled by the retailers, particularly by Amazon.com. Self-publishing production quality can rival that of standard publishing houses. In this context what validates the published work is the audience. If the work is good, it will be purchased. If it is not, then it will not.

When I considered this, I found that the only reason I would want to have a publisher produce my book would be for the bragging rights to say that a big publisher picked me up. In the end, this means that the vanity is in getting a publisher. The tables have turned.

It is not just *difficult* to be nimble with a command and control approach, it is *impossible*. Command and control by definition has long lead times for making decisions. First someone must notice a need for a decision, then they must make others in their line of command aware.

The people on the frontline who notice the need for a decision must communicate the importance and impact to their manager and their manager's manager. All of this takes precious time, time in which your competitor may make a move and cut you out of the market. Yet frontline workers understand the importance and impacts intrinsically because they deal with it every day. If given the authority to make tactical decisions in-line with the business intent, they can respond with lighting speed and the organization can take advantage of these opportunities.

In this paradigm the frontline worker must understand the business far better than they do in most organizations today. Leaders in many organizations do not believe that their frontline people actually have the ability to understand the business. This is a throwback to Fredrick W. Taylor's view of workers. Workers today have a strong desire to be connected with the purpose of the business and to understand the drivers.

Chapter Summary

Business advantage in the knowledge economy stems from innovation and the ability to get that innovation to market quickly. Today's markets change quickly, and the very foundation upon which the industries are built are fundamentally different than anything that has existed before. The primary driver for *agility* is speed. If businesses do not keep up they will be left behind; and by left behind, I mean they will go out of business. It is that simple.

No market is safe from change. Unfortunately, the predominant management approach which was developed at the start of the 20th Century focused primarily upon making workers more efficient and removing them from the need to think. This management approach is no longer viable, and is actually the opposite of what knowledge workers need. Knowledge workers need a new management approach, one that promotes thinking and gives them the responsibility and authority to make decisions in nearly every aspect of the business.

Our current systems of working are not just getting the results we are currently getting but they are optimized to get them. Linear, sequential long duration projects are inappropriate in a context that calls for quick adaptation, experimentation and learning. Agility is what is needed. Not *agile*, the noun that has formed around a set of values and principles for software development.

If you are sensing a theme in this book so far, it is that there is no one-size-fits-all solution for becoming agile. Every organization has a unique set of challenges and opportunities. The most important thing in your organization is engaging your people. In the next chapter, we will explore how your organization's business context impacts how agile you can become.

Selected Resources

Distributed decision making

> Marquet, David (2014) *Turn the Ship Around!: A True Story of Turning Followers into Leaders*, New York, NY: Portfolio Hardcover

> *David Marquet's talk on Greatness!*
> http://bit.ly/distributed_decisions

> *Joseph Flahiff's article* <u>We Don't Do That Here</u>: *Moving from the 3Cs to being a FIT organization.*
> http://www.infoq.com/articles/dont-do-that-here

Action Plan

Now What?

Take a look at your culture. Is your organization trying to optimize for the Industrial Revolution or for knowledge work? As a leader, you can directly impact your part of the organization and you can influence the rest of the organization by publicizing your successes. The goal of this chapter is to help you:

Think

You can probably see now how different engagement looks from command and control. Consider your working style. Think about the interactions with your teammates over the past week or two. Were you a command and control leader or a servant leader?

Act

For the next week, be mindful of how you lead your team. Are you telling people what to do or are you leading them into deeper connection with the business by asking them to step up and make recommendations instead of waiting for answers. Even better, are you asking them to take ownership of their work and letting them make decisions? It is hard to do this to begin with, but with deliberate practice you can get better.

Share

In the last chapter you committed to sharing with two or more people. Now it is time to get some others thinking about what kind of management culture you are going to have in your organization. Have deliberate conversations with people in your organization to discuss the management culture. Start meeting regularly with your peer leaders to discuss these things. If they don't have a copy of the book, encourage them to get one so you can learn together and grow your organization.

Agility in Context

Agility should look different: organization to organization, context to context. There is no one-size-fits-all.

Introduction

> *Context: the circumstances that form the setting for an event, statement, or idea, and in terms of which it can be fully understood and assessed.*

Over the years I have worked with numerous organizations, and with various implementations and interpretations of agility. Through these experiences I have come to categorize these organizations with some wide generalizations:

- Mixed organizations
- Agile organizations
- Non-agile organizations

All are valid implementations and receive value from becoming nimble. Organizations that are not agile at all and do not believe that they need to be agile are few and far between, but there are some. Yet even non-agile organizations can learn from the Agile Movement. Concepts like: servant leadership, collaboration, teamwork and respect are all things the Agile Movement has made central and that can benefit any organization.

Each of these organizational types is different. Their goals, benefits, drivers, trade-offs, and challenges differ significantly. There is so much difference that it is surprising that more people don't talk about this variation. I find that many agilists believe any and all organizations should be completely agile, no matter what business they are in. They fail to see, however, the value in addressing the mixed agile and waterfall contexts.

This may be you! You may be in an organization that seemingly doesn't have a prayer of becoming agile. From the CEO down, there is just no way. Well to you I say, "There is hope!"

When consultants focus on complete organizational transformation, they leave a large swath of people, *maybe you,* with little or no hope. The belief seems to be that either your organization becomes completely agile from top to bottom, or you are doomed. So mixed agile/waterfall organizations are marginalized. I find that mixed nimble and sequential models can fit perfectly well. How agile your organization chooses to become is up to the organization.

Additionally, many people who I speak with only consider a fast and complete agile transformation. A fast transformation can only mean the implementation of business practices and technical processes. Leadership and culture are NOT able to be quickly transformed. It is only with time and concerted effort that any organization can change culture and leadership.

The Big Four: Technical Practices, Business Processes, Culture and Leadership are explained and addressed in detail in Chapter 5.

I understand the desire to make a quick change. It seems similar to ripping off a Band-Aid®. The old ways of working are painful, especially when you have seen new and better ways. As someone who works with people, I desire to help them and not see them in pain any longer. I want to make the change quick and reduce the pain. Rip off the Band-Aid. But organizational change isn't as simple because it needs to include change in culture and leadership. In my experience, slow agile transformation is best. But a slow transformation is hard. It takes focus and a continual effort on the part of the organization's leadership to change the way of working and the organization's culture.

What is a completely agile organization?

Let's take a few minutes and discuss what I mean when I say "completely nimble." I do not mean to imply that there is some destination that an organization will reach, a state where they are *done* with working on agility. This is a fairly common, although not explicit, misconception. Somehow people believe that they will *do an agile transformation* and then, *poof*, they are agile. Agility is like being physically fit. You have to continually work at it. Diets don't work for one simple reason. If you go on a diet, there is an implicit expectation that it is a temporary event of some duration after which life will get *back to normal*, and you will remain fit. But that isn't how being physically fit works. What you really need is a *lifestyle change*. You have to make eating well and exercise a part of your life, something you enjoy and would never think of giving up. It becomes your *new normal*. Becoming agile works the same way. It is a continual process of refinement and improvement. This journey is not one where a simple destination is reached and then things *return to normal*. Continuous improvement *is* the new normal.

The next step in becoming a completely agile organization is moving to a place where you are able to keep pace with the changes. An organization could conceivably reach this point by simply instituting some business processes and technical practices that enable agility. Unfortunately this may, in the long term, be a state of *tenuous agility*. It is tenuous if the *organizational culture and leadership* have not been explicitly designed to be supportive of agility. The gravity of the old ways of doing things will constantly pull the organization back and the agile cohort will need to continually resist that pull.

If an organization is going to become completely agile, then cultural and leadership change is necessary. Only when leadership and the culture they create are altered will the whole system be self-perpetuating.

The Long Dry Middle

The most sustainable transformations are a combination of some quick changes and slow patient evolution of the leadership and culture.

Historically, agile adoption has been bottom up. In practice these moves typically start with a pocket of agility. A group within the organization somewhere, usually a web team in the IT department, decides to try Scrum. This group has some success and news spreads. Other groups within the IT organization try it. Pretty soon there are enough groups that management takes notice. If management is forward thinking enough and does not feel threatened by the egalitarian nature of Scrum, then they get on-board. Leadership starts to see the benefits and becomes supportive. Then it jumps departments and divisions. Over time, more and more of the organization becomes supportive of being agile.

There were several big leaps in there. One of the most significant was the leap from one department or division to another.

Sometimes the relationships between departments or divisions in an organization are, shall we say..., less than friendly. Leaders in organizations large and small build kingdoms for themselves, and they are not quick to give these up. Most agile enabling technical practices and business processes use cross functional teams that frequently cut across kingdom lines. Cutting across boundaries is great for delivery, but not so good for keeping your kingdom together. When this happens, the effort is often either stopped at the boundary of the kingdom or it gets squashed out of fear that the kingdom the leader took so long to create is threatened.

In either case, it is imperative that the leader be carefully educated about the value of teaming, collaboration and cooperation.

Positioning them as a leader in the organization is one possible approach to obtaining their consent. However, getting their consent and willingness to learn a supportive servant leadership approach are two very different things.

This is the middle time - the stretch when the organization is struggling to become agile. Not everyone in the organization knows what agile is; or if they do know what it is, they may not believe it is a valid approach. There are myths and misinformation about agility. This can be a frustrating and long period of time. Unfortunately, it isn't given a lot of thought or written about much. These long dry middle organizations will be addressed with other organizations that are a combination of agile and non-agile.

Mixed Agile/Non-Agile

What about organizations that will never be agile across the board, where agile and waterfall have to coexist? The United States Federal Government, for example, will always have some part that is waterfall. We cannot get away from the elections, terms, and sessions of the Congress, which drive some element of sequential, non-agile cycles. Can the United States federal, state and local governments benefit from being agile in parts and waterfall in others? YES! *Emphatically YES!*

When coaching or meeting with a team for the first time, they describe their situation and then I ask if they are agile. Often they don't know what they even mean when they say agile. They heard that they need to be agile. They made some technical practice or business process changes; and then they want to know if they are there yet. *There is no one-size-fits-all. Agility should look different: organization to organization, context to context.*

Online Extra

Austin's Butterfly: Take a few minutes away from this book to watch this video:

http://bit.ly/austins_bu tterfly .

I show the video *Austin's Butterfly* (see Online Extra) to clients to illustrate a number of important points. Here I want to focus on the butterfly itself.

When did it become a butterfly? I think you will agree that it became a butterfly the first time Austin drew it. However, each time he tried again he drew a better butterfly. Similarly, when we first decide to become agile we put our feet upon the road and we are in the process of becoming agile. Because it is difficult to actually calculate what the rate of change is in any given industry, it is difficult to say exactly when an organization crosses that border and becomes agile.

How far you go down the road, how much of your organization becomes agile, how much remains sequential/waterfall will all differ from organization to organization.

Types of organizations

The Agile Movement began in the software industry. In this section we will talk for a bit about software to illustrate the point. But then we will expand this thinking beyond these limitations. So, if you are not in software, hang with me. This will apply to you once we broaden the topic at the end of the chapter.

Let's slice the world into two kinds of organizations. Those who produce software as its primary product, we will call *Software Product organizations* (SPO). The other type of company is one where the primary product is something else, and software is a supporting service. We will call these *Software Supported organizations* (SSO).

Examples of SPOs include:

- Microsoft
- Adobe
- Amazon
- Expedia

These companies either sell the software as the product or, their primary or only sales channel is through software.

By contrast, SSOs do not essentially *need* the software. If there was a different way of providing the service that software provides, the company would not appear any different to the customer. Likewise, if the underlying software support were to radically change (e.g. from in-house mainframes, to personal computers, to cloud based service, or some other form), the customers would see no difference at all in the company.

Examples of software supported/hybrid organizations include:

- Geico Insurance
- Gibson Guitars
- Toyota Motor Company
- Your local grocery chain

At first glance it may appear that there is not a significant difference between SSOs and SPOs because in many of the SSOs software is a huge part of the product they sell. Insurance is one example. The primary product an insurance company sells is a sense of security created by having insurance to cover emergency situations, but there are massive software support systems that support the organization. If the calculations executed by the software support services go down and the company has to calculate the insurance statistics and payments by hand, the business would look no different to the end user. Customers still receive their sense of security. Contrast this with Amazon. If the software at Amazon goes down, there is no Amazon.

Impact of Organizational Type on Ease of Transformation

In organizations where software is the primary product, introducing and using agile is much more straightforward than in software supported organizations. In SPOs the use of a role such as *Product Owner* is not a stretch. The role of product owner, and even the title, likely already exists. They exist as someone's full time position in the organization, often filled by a senior person who knows the product that is being produced inside and out. This role is natural and normal at a software company. One telltale sign that the product owner is a real full time position is that it exists, as a title, on the *organizational chart*.

The focus and, therefore, process of the SPO is completely different. The software that the organization sells is always considered in light of a lifetime of releases. Each release is followed by the next in a never ending sequence of improvement and feature additions. The organization structures itself wholly round such a mindset. When taken in the context of a product, rather than a project, the agile concepts of the product backlog make perfect sense, even if the organization is not using an agile approach yet. Since the product exists as a series of releases, each with continual improvement and enhancement, then adding or subtracting from the current release is a much simpler task than considering a software release a project, with a limited and fixed scope, schedule and budget.

The focus of the push for agility has much to do with how smooth the implementation will be and how pervasive it will become. Most organizations are built with a hierarchical structure.

The Product Owner

The role of Product Owner is critical to the success of an agile move in both SPOs and SSOs. Let's look more deeply at the product owner in his or her natural habitat, a software product organization.

In a SPO - The Product Owner in a software product organization is responsible for the success of the product. Since software is the primary product of the company, the product owner is also responsible for the success of the company. Their vision and direction are visible to the highest levels of the organization. They likely report directly to CxO level executives. They are involved in the most critical discussions within the organization regarding business direction, and their decisions are supported by the senior executive levels. They have budgetary responsibility for the product, both for the expenses *and for the revenue*. They are often directly compensated though bonuses and other benefits for the success or failure of the product. Basically when the PO says, "Jump!", the organization asks, "How high?"

In a SSO - On the contrary, in a software supported organization the role of Product Owner does not typically exist on the organization chart. If the role exists at all, it is because an agile group has required it and it is, typically, assigned to someone in addition to the group's existing work. Actually, there often is no single Product Owner but a number of people, each of whom has a part interest in the product. We frequently find the role of

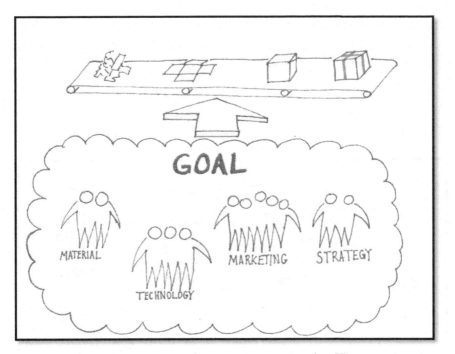

Product Owner is assigned to someone in the IT organization. Most often, it is assigned to the person who is responsible for supporting the product in production. This person, however, does not have budgetary control for the product. They are not responsible for the expenses or revenue generated. They do not have the ear of executive leadership, and they are not compensated for the success or failure of the product. In short, they do not have the power or authority to make decisions about the product. Then there are all of the other people who have a say in the product. Each department that uses it will have some pull on the requirements and some say in what is important. When this PO says, "Jump!", the organization asks, "Why?"

Additionally, the SSO Product Owner is only a part time Product Owner; thus I find that they often do not have enough time to spend on the responsibilities and duties that are necessary to do the full time job of Product Owner. They are busy managing 15 other products because they are a software support manager, not a product line manager. They spend much of their time focused

on other important duties within the organization. Supporting the software for the company is after all their job.

Finally, I find that Product Owners in SSOs, when they are assigned from the management in IT, are most often not very knowledgeable about the business use and needs of the product or the requirements of the users. This is, again, understandable as the person's primary role is to keep the wheels of the IT organization running - maintaining the numerous software and hardware systems that are required by the organization and developing the IT staff who report to them. It is no wonder they do not have the time to research the needs and understand how every products' customers work.

Product Delivery

In a SPO the entire organization is focused upon the delivery of the product. Every department supports the delivery of the product, from accounting to HR, from sales and marketing to operations and support. The view of the product is a long term *product management* approach. The success of the product is equated with the success of the organization. Likewise, the failure of the product is equated to the failure of the business.

An SSO is most often operated in the *project management* mindset as opposed to a product management mindset. With a projectized organization, each year projects are evaluated individually, based on a new business case, a new charter and a new budget. Each project is evaluated against all of the other projects proposed for the organization. Only those projects deemed important enough are approved and allocated budgets. That means, if a system that was developed or enhanced last year has features that were not completed within the project, those features are not guaranteed to be included in the subsequent year or years. There may be other systems that are more important to the overall success of the company, and the financial resources of the organization will be allocated to these other systems. This is as it should be! The focus of this organization is the sale of some other product or service, not the software. The software is merely a support service like any other support service such as accounting or HR. If the money will serve the sale of the business' primary product or service better by being spent on something else, then it should be. In this context, the agile process of product backlog management is more complicated because projects by definition have a specific scope. Some items are in that scope and some items are out of that scope.

Scope

Consider the software giant Microsoft and the product *Windows*. Way back in the day, Microsoft began releasing its Windows product with Windows 3.1. This was a revolutionary product for the PC market using a graphical user interface rather than a command line interface that MS-DOS used. Soon after the release of Windows 3.1 was the release of Windows 3.11. The difference between the two was primarily the addition of peer to peer networking. Why was this released in a .01 addition to the Windows product? It was released because it just didn't make it into the 3.1 release. Microsoft's Windows team simply rolled into the next release because there was a next release.

Product management is considered a long term thing with on-going budgets. In contrast, project management is a one-time event to create a unique product service or result. This difference should not be taken lightly.

If Windows had been considered a project, and networking was part of the original scope, then the Windows 3.1 project would have been considered a failure because it did not include networking. We would never have seen Windows peer to peer networking because project budgets are one-time events, when they are gone they are gone and they do not automatically recur.

Product budgets are an annual thing. If a feature does not make this release, it is not absolutely fatal for that feature as it will make it into the next release.

Does this mean you cannot use agile for project work on an annual budget cycle? By no means, but let's explore the issue a little further before we talk about how to do it.

Schedule

Like scope, schedules for a SPO are viewed differently than schedules for SPO.

The Project Management Institute (PMI) defines a project as "A temporary endeavor undertaken to create a unique product service or result." As such, it has a defined beginning and a defined end. Often these defined ends are fixed and, in theory, immovable. So, for the typical project all of the scope must be delivered within a fixed, sometimes arbitrary, schedule. *At this point it is important to point out that agile works very well on projects that are part of a product being delivered in iterations. In this case agile appears to work with fixed projects. The defining difference is that in a typical non-software project, there is no next release, and all of the scope must be completed within the given schedule and quite often for the allocated budget.*

It may appear that there is no problem with this approach; yet the problem lies, not so much in that the schedule is fixed, but that a standalone project limits the possible responses. What are your responses when scope is added? 1) Remove other, lower value scope from the current release and put it into the next release; or 2) Move out the schedule for the current release to accommodate the additional scope. Well, in the case of a standalone project, there is no *next release*.

Budget

Now consider how budgets are handled in a project vs. a product management context.

In a SPO – Budgets for a product are cyclical. As a Product Owner for a software product, I know that I will have a new budget next year for the product. It may be increased or decreased but it will be there; or I should be looking for another job because the product line is going to go away.

In a SSO – Project budgets contrast with product budgets in that they are typically allocated once and for a fixed amount. The budget is allocated at a corporate planning session where all of the work for the organization is balanced against all of the other work in the organization. The budget is allocated for the work and that is it. The entire scope of the work is supposed to be completed within that budget and no other budget is expected or planned. The ability of a product to roll from one release to another is thus again limited if the budget is limited.

Summary of Scope Schedule and Budget

So what do you do? It seems that on every side enterprise projects are not fit for agile delivery. But it's not all there is to the story. There is a lot that we can do even with these limitations. One key to successfully executing agile or lean for a project is to be aware of the limitations of the context in which you are operating. Your teams will likely not be aware of the limitations that projects place on many agile practices. If they have not heard of these limitations, then they may need your help to understand what is and is not reasonable in a project environment that is not based in a product line. The contextual limitations of your organization must still be respected and their implications on the potential agility of your project understood.

	Project Management	*Product Management*
Scope	Fixed set of features	On-going prioritized list of features
Schedule	Start and end date	Multiple releases
Budget	Allocated once	Cyclical

Can Software Supported Organizations be agile?

Is all this to say then that SSOs cannot be agile? By no means! The vast majority of my time is spent with SSOs, helping them to become agile. But it is to say that you must be aware of the challenges presented by your organizational structure. If you do not understand these issues, you will be constantly surprised by problems you should have expected all along. Also, be aware that the agility of a software supported, projectized organization will look different from agility in a software product company. The rest of this book talks about some baby steps into agile that you can take in a SSO.

Beyond Software

This chapter has spoken mostly about software because software is where the majority of organizations start with their explorations into agility. Let's broaden the picture now to include everyone because today I find that moves for agility can start anywhere in the organization, not just in software.

In some organizations agility begins in the core product or service. This implementation will reflect the characteristics of a SPO. In other organizations it begins as a pocket of agility and never grows beyond that. The important thing to consider is the sphere of influence of the organization that is pushing for agility. If it is a small pocket waaayyyyy down in a support department, any major organizational change, agile or whatever, isn't going to carry the same weight as it would if it were coming from the top down.

This brings up a good point. As I said when we discussed *The Long Dry Middle*, agile adoption has historically been a grassroots thing. Unfortunately, organizational silos have significantly hampered the potential scope of success for these attempts. In more recent times, changes have been what Mike Orzen, author of <u>Lean IT</u>, calls "Bottom Up, Top Enabled." The effort is still grassroots but it has full support from the top of the organization. The CxO level is engaged and supportive of the move toward agility, however, they are not forcing it on anyone. They are letting it organically grow and supporting the changes. A bottom up top enabled approach can begin in a small pocket but because of the support of the top, it has the possibility to grow beyond the silo where it started. You don't have to start out top enabled. You can gain that over time. In many organizations a pocket of agility proves its success and gains the attention of upper management.

Take heart if you are in a mixed agile and waterfall context and you don't see how the organization could ever move beyond it. Just do your best, improve where you can improve within your scope of authority, and make the barriers that are in the way visible. Do not judge others in the organization or put them down for not being agile. Believe that they just don't know yet because it is hard to see how something so new, something so different could apply in their specific, and very different context. Over time, your success coupled with your kindness will create a gravity that will draw people to you.

One thing people often fail to do in the rush to make changes and start working smarter is to track metrics. It is critical to the future of your efforts to track what you are doing, track metrics on what you were doing, and then on how things change when you become agile. Therefore, when you start to see success you can talk in concrete terms about the difference it has made.

Change is a difficult thing. I am more in favor of the approach that is outlined by Chip and Dan Heath in their book Switch: How to Change when Change is Hard. The authors use an analogy of an elephant and a rider. In this relationship the elephant has the power but the rider has the will and wants to direct the elephant in a particular direction. The metaphor explains our brains and motivation. The left brain/logical side needs reasons and logic; the right brain/emotional side needs to be inspired and motivated.

Organizational leaders need to provide both. In their top enable role, they need to provide vision and direction. In Chapter 5 we will discuss a complete approach to organizational transformation including all four aspects of agility.

Chapter Summary

Your organization type, and where in that organization you are, has a significant impact on the way agility is expressed. Organizations considering agility will fall into one or more of three types: Mixed Agile and Waterfall, All Agile, or Non-Agile. It is important to note that all organizations can learn from the Agile Movement and all organizations will benefit from the 21st Century management thinking as discussed in Chapter 1.

Even those organizations that are becoming All Agile will go through a period of being mixed agile and waterfall. For some this is a relatively quick transition, for others it can take years. We call this the Long Dry Middle. During this period, All Agile transformation candidates should consider themselves to be Mixed Agile and Waterfall, for that is what they really are for the time being. This perspective will save you a lot of heartache, wishing, hoping, and believing your organization is or should be something that it isn't yet.

When an agile transformation is driven by the core product or service of the organization, that transformation is much easier than when it is driven from a support services organization. Another key struggle experienced by Mixed Agile and Waterfall organizations is the project vs. product mind-set. Most agility enabling practices are more suited to a product mind-set than a project mind-set

Selected Resources

Creating Culture

Catmull, Ed (2014) *Creativity, Inc.,* New York, NY : Random House

Sheridan, Richard (2014) *Joy Inc.: How We Built a Workplace People Love,* New York, NY: Portfolio Hardcover

Austin's butterfly

http://bit.ly/austins_butterfly

Projects vs. Products. My presentation at the PMI Global Congress in Huston Texas, 2011

http://bit.ly/PMIAgile2011

http://www.infoq.com/articles/agile-in-waterfall-world

Action Plan

Now What?

Understand your context. Are you a Product Organization or a Support Organization? Are you in the *Long Dry Middle* on your way toward somewhere else, but living in a mixed context now? As a leader, you can directly impact your part of the organization and you can influence the rest of the organization by publicizing your successes. The goal of this chapter is to help you understand why your organization, or others you may have heard about, struggle with trying to be agile.

Think

What kind of organization are you in? Are you directly responsible for the profit and loss of a product? Or are you in a support organization? Has this caused frustration in you or in people in your organization when they tried to *do agile*? Now that you understand the trouble that is caused by trying to apply product thinking to a project, consider how you might have responded differently if you had understood these challenges.

Act

Review your existing reporting, documentation, change processes and other tools that are used to track and communicate project information. Do any of these resources limit your ability to be agile? If you have a project or portfolio office, and/or governance structures, review these and consider how they are tied to a command and control mind-set. Review how work is evaluated, funded and approved. Do these processes support or restrict agility? Trying to change these structures may be difficult without careful planning, but it is possible. Within the part of the organization where you can influence, start to build a case for moving to a customer focused product based model of work execution.

Share

In your regularly scheduled meetings with the cohort that you setup in the last chapter, discuss the project/product relationship and what that looks like in your organization. What problems has it caused and how can the group of you help your organization get a better understanding of the complexity of trying to be agile with a fixed budget, scope, and/or schedule.

Variable Agility

There is no one-size-fits-all agility.

Where does agility fit?

There was an interesting question asked by someone who laid sewer lines when I was on a panel of agile experts speaking in Portland, Oregon. He asked if agile applied to his work. What came out of that discussion was that agile means the ability to nimbly shift with changing requirements and new information. It means the agility to adapt to changing environments quickly and easily. But what does *quickly and easily* mean? Is it the same in every context?

For software, defining *quickly and easily* is pretty simple. For example, I was talking with the CTO of an online content site and he shared how nimble you can be with software. When they hire a new person, that new person writes production code and puts it into production the first day they are there. The first day they are there! Can you imagine?! He said, "We want to hire really bright people and really bright people want to code, I mean that is what they are here for." In most companies, the first day, two or three…a week…involves getting a computer, reading the HR manual and doing basically, nothing. This forward thinking CTO says, "Let's put them on the computer and get them working, doing what they love to do and then they will be excited to be here!"

You can be very nimble with software because it's just that way. I can go in the middle of something and change a screen or whatever. But what is agility for a sewer line or an oil pipeline? You can't just say, "Hey, you are new. Go out there and lay some pipe." That is *not* to say the pipeline company cannot get new people working on interesting things right away, but it is different.

The same kind of agility for a pipeline may mean that *quickly* means three months, instead of three hours. A pipeline may take five years to put in. So on a pipeline, maybe three months is what an iteration would be. Maybe three months is what makes you agile in the pipeline or sewer project. It is all a matter of scale.

Let's look at it more generically in the illustration below. If your Build Cycle, shown by the length of the trucks, is longer than your industry Change Cycle, shown by the space between people, then you definitely need to become more agile. The reason for this is that by the time you get your product or service to market it is out of date and the industry has moved on to something new and better.

Note that the horizontal timeline has no markers demarking specific time *scale*. It is not the *scale* that makes you agile it is the *relationship* between the Change Cycle and the Delivery Cycle that makes you agile.

If your Build Cycles are shorter than your industry Change Cycle, then you may not need to change anything, even if you are using a sequential approach to delivery. I know that is heresy in some agile circles to say you could actually be agile and execute sequentially. But if your sequential delivery results in agility, then who cares. It is not how you execute that makes you agile, but the relationship between your Delivery Cycle and your Change Cycle.

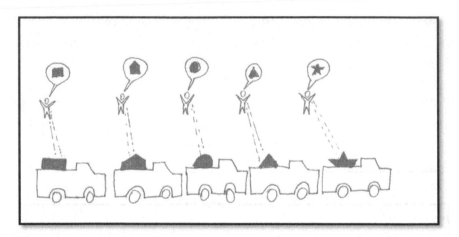

That said, there is still much that any business can stand to learn from the *Agile Movement, 21st Century Management Thinking and the new Agile Enabling Practices*. Not all of these are limited to organizations that need or are agile, much of them are just good for business.

Being agile is critically important to many industries. Delivering high quality, satisfying stakeholders and customers, and producing products more quickly with less rework are good for *any* business, in *any* industry, *anywhere*.

Agility Horizons

Since I am from Seattle, and Boeing is located here, I guess it is natural for me to talk about the building of airliners. An airliner is a thing by itself with a plan for construction, milestones and specific dependencies. When a business orders a new jetliner, it is constructed and built according to the agreed upon specifications.

That is all true, but it can also be thought of as a system of systems. These systems include the guidance systems, propulsion systems, directional control, air circulation, the back of the seat televisions, the lavatories, and many more. Each of these systems in turn is also a system of systems. The guidance systems on a superliner consist of hundreds, even thousands of separate but interdependent systems.

Why all this talk about systems? The reason is this. These systems all have their own specific technologies, each with its own technology change cycles. If the propulsion system has a change cycle of 18 months. That is to say that new technological innovations take 18 months to develop, then the agile horizon for this technology is 18 months. That means you better be able to incorporate new changes into your products every 18 or fewer months or someone else is going to do it and leave you behind.

If on the other hand the flight guidance system has a change cycle of three months, then its agile horizon is three months. Your organization better be able to adopt the new systems every three months or you are going to be left behind. And don't tell me that *it can't be done;* someone is going to do it. That is what innovation is all about. If innovation is happening on a horizon of three months, you darn well better be adopting it or some other organization is going to make it happen.

In designing a system of systems like a jetliner, it is important then to keep in mind that the critical component is the interface between systems. The contract between these two systems must be made as simple as possible, and robust as necessary. Additionally, the interdependencies between systems must be kept to a bare minimum to allow each technology to have its change cycle and not impact the overall working of the larger system.

Mixing agile and waterfall

Ok, let's pull up out of the minutia for a minute for a specific example. From design to delivery, a jetliner can take anywhere from 5 to 10 years. If I ordered one of these awesome vehicles, and it arrived with a guidance and control system that was 10 years old…I would quickly ask for my money back. But didn't I order a jet that was designed 5-10 years ago? Shouldn't I expect it to have old technology? Of course not, but why? Because the designers of jets know that they need to loosely couple these systems in order to make sure that the aircraft keeps pace with the updates in technology and safety. If these interfaces are kept clean and robust, it allows the underlying technology to adapt to changes without impacting the integrity of the overall system(s). It becomes clear then that in any industry close attention must be paid to the interfaces between systems in order to maximize the overall agility of a non-agile system.

When you have *loosely coupled modules* *with clearly defined interfaces* you reduce the risk of the project because you are reducing the interdependence between the modules. Notice that they are not completely independent, but the dependency is reduced. This way you are able to make changes to one sub-system of the larger system without impacting the whole system. It sounds simple but the ramifications are significant. Consider the cost of retesting all of the sub-systems when you make one small change versus testing one sub-system and ensuring that the interface remained unchanged.

This is a different way of thinking about how systems are architected. The Wikispeed car is a perfect example of how this principle can be applied and the dramatic impact it can have. I am not a car guy. But I know enough to share this example. All cars have some kind of suspension system. Two types are the McPherson Strut system and a Double Wishbone system. The effort to change from one system of suspension to the other on nearly every automobile is significant. It entails essentially reconstructing the entire undercarriage of the vehicle, which takes weeks.

But not for the Wikispeed car. The Wikispeed car was created with this architectural principle. As a result, to change from one suspension system to the other takes about ten minutes. It involves just six bolts. Unbolt six bolts, take off the suspension plate, install the next suspension plate, and tighten the bolts.

The same approach applies to the engine. Imagine the benefits of this. The Wikispeed car was built for the Automotive X Prize race. If there was some new, dramatic improvement in engine technology the week before the race, then the innovators working on the Wikispeed car would be able to create a new engine and install it by unbolting the old engine and sliding it out, sliding in the new engine and bolting it in just before the race. The other competitors with traditional, integrated modules would not be able to take advantage of the new battery technology because their systems are all integrated with one another.

Is Waterfall Still Relevant?

At this point I think it is important to address a common misconception in the agile world that waterfall or sequential project delivery is bad, evil, irrelevant, and is going to disappear in *the pure bright blinding light of an agile epiphany!*

I hear this when I speak and attend agile events around the world, and on blogs and discussion groups. The belief is now that we have agile, no projects need waterfall anymore, because agile is so much better.

It is very true *for the people who are saying it*; becoming agile has improved their projects, their success and, yes, their lives. Their projects actually deliver, giving them insight into what is really happening. In general, taking an agile approach makes way more sense than sequential project management ever did for them. But does that mean sequential/plan driven/waterfall delivery is bad? This is a false dichotomy. Taking a plan driven approach logically makes sense sometimes.

I was the IT infrastructure Project Manager for the construction of the Seattle Cancer Care Alliance Building in Seattle. The Alliance was created to bring the patient treatment practices of the University of Washington, the Seattle Children's Hospital and the Fred Hutchinson Cancer Research Center together. The most important thing to these organizations was the *successful eradication of cancer in their patients. Or as the Hutch puts it, "The mission of Fred Hutchinson Cancer Research Center is the elimination of cancer and related diseases as causes of human suffering and death."*

Clearly treating patients is important to this mission. Parking, on the other hand, is nowhere to be found in the mission statements of any of the partner organizations. Therefore, it follows that the patient registration on the first floor and the treatment facility on the second floor are significantly more important than parking. If we were designing a website, we could have created the highest value item first. But since we were creating a physical building, there were significantly more sequential dependencies. The parking was beneath the building. Therefore, the parking needed to be built first. And the next floor after that and the next floor after that. There was no delivering the second floor first, then going back and delivering the parking later, even though from a priority standpoint the floors were more important.

Agile or waterfall?

Amy Edmonson, in her book ***Teaming: How Organizations Learn, Innovate, and Compete in the Knowledge Economy***, introduces the concept of *The Process Knowledge Spectrum* to describe a spectrum of how much is known about a particular piece of work and the processes necessary to do work. At the one extreme is everyday normal work, Routine Operations. This work and the processes necessary to do it are well known. At the other extreme of the Process Knowledge Spectrum is Innovative Work. This work is new and exploratory. It has never been attempted before, thus neither the work nor the processes necessary to do the work are known. In the middle, Amy places Complex Work. When we look at our delivery approach in light of this model, we can see that when there is a lot of process knowledge, we *can* be somewhat more predictive in our approach. Similarly, when there is a less known approach, we *must* be more adaptive (agile).

Clearly there are areas where a more sequential approach is perfectly valid and should be the preferred method. It should be preferred when the sequence and dependencies are well known. There is no value in iterating on work that is clearly defined. Setting up systems that enable iteration actually add waste in overhead that could be avoided because the system process knowledge is high. In construction, it is well known how long it takes to put in a wall: studs, sheetrock, tape, prime and paint. There is no point in setting up feedback cycles and iterating on the installation of the wall. If on the other hand, we were installing a wall using materials or methods that were unknown (low process knowledge), then it makes perfect sense to iterate and get feedback in quick cycles to make sure we are on the right path.

Yes but...

We have shown that it is true in some cases that a sequential approach may be preferable. However, let's not forget the first chapter of this book. Beware of implementations that are too long in cycle; your industry may just change overnight.

I am reminded of some construction in our neighbourhood back in early 2008. There were about 35 tract homes being built down the road from my house. The builder had high process knowledge of the construction of tract houses. So he was on the Routine Operations side of the Process Knowledge Spectrum. What the builder didn't understand was Lean and the concept of large batch size and inventory waste. People choose large batch size because of the incorrect belief that since there are fewer changeovers there is savings with large batches. Large batches take a long time to process. Because large batches take so long to process and you end up having a lot of partially completed inventory (that is worthless until it is completed), this is a huge risk. This is one of the reasons that Taiichi Ohno of Toyota identified inventory as one of the seven wastes to be eliminated. This builder learned this lesson the hard way. When the debt market crashed, the builder was left with eight or nine houses in a half built state. If they had built one house at a time, they would have been left with 10 or 12 completed houses. The rest of the lots would have remained empty. The completed houses could have at least been rented out or sold. As it was, the houses sat vacant until 2011 when the housing market recovered enough to make it desirable to complete the houses.

Yes and...

Just because you are delivering in a sequential manner does not mean that you are exempt from needing 21st Century management thinking, such as servant leadership, respecting people, engagement and distributed decision making. We understand more about people and our motivations than we did during the Industrial Revolution. It is important that we put this knowledge to work and not rely on managing through fear, command and control. For example, there is no reason you cannot be a servant leader on a sequential project.   There is also no reason you cannot have self-organizing teams that are empowered to create the plan and take on the work they plan and estimate. I remember well when I was working on the Seattle Cancer Care Alliance project, and it was time to create the initial project plan. Yes, it was a Gantt chart.   But I didn't do it. I got the team together and had them brainstorm the process and sequence of the work. They knew better than I did as to what they planned to do. Yes, I facilitated the planning, but I didn't do the planning myself. When that was done, they all knew what their roles were and what they would be responsible for because they had come up with it!

My role then turned to one of serving the team to make it as smooth as possible for them to do the work that they had defined for themselves.   I was a cheerleader, a roadblock remover, a water carrier, and a gofer to help them get the job done. I handled the hard discussions and confrontations that needed to happen when conflict arose. I took the heat. This is your role.

The *all projects will become agile* argument is actually falling into the same fallacy that was preached in the 80s/90s to software. Now, that shoe is on the other foot. Back then the traditional (waterfall) project management approach used in construction and the military was applied to software development. Now, the agile world is saying that what they have found successful should be applied to all other projects. They have not considered that there are projects, such as construction, where having a detailed plan in advance helps tremendously.

Chapter Summary

As it says in the chapter subtitle, there is no one-size-fits-all agility. Every organization is unique, and every expression of agility is likewise, unique. Determining your best expression of agility means finding your agility horizon and shortening your delivery cycle to be less than that horizon.

With this definition it is easy to see that mixing agile and waterfall is actually done all the time. The key is to create *loosely coupled modules with clearly defined interfaces.* By architecting systems in this way you will reduce current and future risks and you will reduce testing cost/time.

Waterfall is still relevant but likely in fewer arenas than you might think. Understanding where your work sits on the process knowledge spectrum and with our expanded understanding of agility, work that may have appeared to be waterfall is actually just long cycle agile work. Be careful not to confuse your agility horizon with large batch work.

Really most important of all is to understand that no work, no organization is exempt from needing 21st Century thinking practices like servant leadership, respecting people, engagement and distributed decision making!

Selected Resources

Amy Edmonson (2012) *Teaming: How organizations learn, innovate and compete in the knowledge economy*, New York, NY: Jossey Bass

Wikispeed:

http://wikispeed.org/

Your Action Plan

Now What

I hope that by this point agility is becoming clearer to you. Mixing an agile approach and sequential/waterfall approach is not that difficult when we demystify them.

Think

Look carefully at your organization and your projects. Are they all using the same agility horizon? If so, do they need to use the same one? What is your context? Do you have a long or a short change cycle? Do you know? Take some time to analyze your organization and determine your agility horizon. Do you have nested agility needs? Is your organization operating with 20th Century management thinking or 21st Century management thinking?

Act

If you have not already done so, and most people have not, your action for this chapter is to begin gathering data regarding the frequency of change in your organization. Do not limit yourself to things like approved change requests, but look deeper to the frequency of change inquiries. This will give you a good idea of your maximum agility horizon. You can always have a shorter horizon but you should never have a longer horizon than your change cycle.

Share

As you gather this information about your agility horizon, start talking about it with your co-workers. You have already engaged some in conversations about your organization's need for agility.   Have they ever heard of agility horizons? What do they think about the idea of nested agility and could they see it used in your organization?

Start having deliberate discussions about where your various work lies on the process knowledge spectrum. Is it known work that has set processes, or is it innovative work that needs a more exploratory model? Draw this information into your discussions of agility horizons. How does your process knowledge impact your agility horizons? Most important of all, start discussing how you can begin creating 21st Century management thinking. (Additional suggestions will be introduced in Chapter 6.)

The Big Four

A framework for understanding approach to organizational change

Introduction

Pick up any business periodical and you will find article after article about the rapid rate of change, the constant need for innovation, the need for business to be agile, nimble, flexible and adaptable. Moore's law stated that technology basically doubles every two years. If you want to have some real fun, go check out http://thesingularity.com. The concept of the singularity is that moment when the sum of technology will surpass the sum of human knowledge. While I don't subscribe to the implication of the site, it is fun to see all the hockey-stick curves.

There is no doubt that being nimble is necessary to today's business, but is your organization agile? Is your organization able to adapt to change? Can you sustainably maintain this state of agility indefinitely?

Yesterday, I met with a client whose company recently spent over a million dollars on a multinational agile initiative, and today they have nothing to show for it. I shared the four aspects of agility with her. As I suspected, they had only addressed the top two: technical practices and business processes.

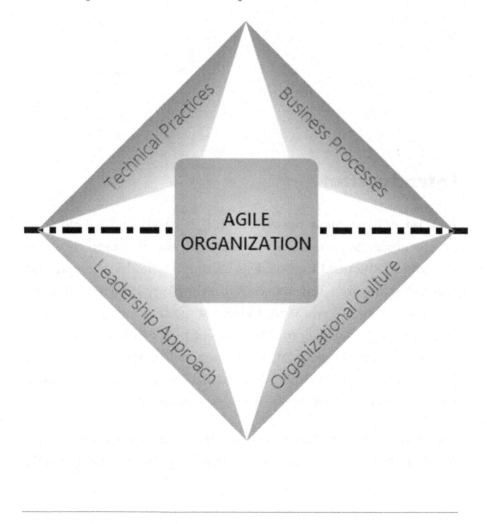

This is not an uncommon problem because the top two are the easier of the aspects to address. They can be taught, developed, and operationalized. They should be handled carefully because any change in an organization can be difficult and emotionally challenging. In the study of Behavioral Economics, a study of how behaviors affect financial decisions, the research shows that people, to a disproportionate degree, when given the choice of better alternatives, will choose to do nothing - keep the status quo.

According to John P. Kotter, author of Leading Change, neuroscience shows that the emotional side of our thinking is more firmly rooted than our logical thinking side. If large scale organizational change is going to be successful, it needs to focus on the cultural and emotional side. The bottom two aspects of agility: organizational culture and leadership approach are not something that can be taught; they must be developed with time, diligence and patience. Cultural change and organizational leadership change take significant effort from those in management.

Do your technical practices and business processes, your culture and leadership approach support being nimble? If you haven't made a *specific effort* to create a sustainable balance in your agile organization, the answer is likely, "No."

Every organization is a complex adaptive system. Complex systems are those where cause and effect are not directly related, such that it is impossible to determine the outcome of any particular action. This is often because the systems are so complex that it is impossible to account for every nuance. There may be an element of chance or chaos that is also a part of the system. You probably have heard this kind of system referred to as the *butterfly effect*. The butterfly effect is the idea that a butterfly flapping its wings in Ghana can cause a hurricane in the Gulf of Mexico through a series of small and large interconnected but unseen events.

In these complex systems, patterns of outcomes are observable, and probable predictions can be made on those patterns. However, direct cause and effect are obfuscated. An adaptive system is one that continually adapts to the environment. A Complex Adaptive System is a system of systems that is not able to be directly predicted. Patterns emerge, however, that are predictable, and those patterns are constantly adapting to the system's environment.

A lack of understanding of the basic nature of complexity leads to numerous misunderstandings. For example, people try to oversimplify complex systems like macroeconomics, healthcare in the United States, politics, the dynamic relationships of departments and divisions in an organization, and even interpersonal relationships.

The place you work is a Complex Adaptive System (CAS). We are uncomfortable with things we don't understand. We try to form rules and make the complex understandable. We assign causality where none exists. We institute policies and procedures not really recognizing that even those policies and procedures are little more than another layer in the CAS.

When giving a workshop, to illustrate the unseen interconnectedness of everything, I will often ask the whole class to stand up. I then tell each person to pick two people in the room without making any indication of whom they have chosen. Once I say, "Go," I have the people place themselves equidistance between the two people. As you can imagine, chaos ensues. Normally the shifting and swirling of people will not stop. Once in a while it finds a balance point, and then I move one person and the whole thing starts again. It is a lot of fun, but the purpose of the exercise is to illustrate the point that we have no idea how interconnected our organizations are. So, be careful when you make any change in your organization. Your system may be at a point where it has found stability, and trying an idea discussed in this book will likely have implications you didn't expect. Don't be discouraged; just be aware that things are interrelated. When you try something, carefully observe the results and then modify your approach. Don't try too many things at once. Just like in a science experiment, you only change one variable at a time so you can be more confident that changes you observe in the system are the result of the experiment you tried.

In an *adaptive system,* the systems interact and work together to create a greater system that is actually more than the sum of its parts. Sort of like the way physics can describe bosons, leptons, neutrons, atoms, molecules, cells, and tissues. But a living person is more than the sum of those elements. They are the constituent parts but not the whole story. This could get really theoretical really fast. While I really do enjoy exploring these higher level discussions, they often don't help us on the practical day-to-day.

Back to the practical. Your organization is a complex system of systems. Which, when they all work together in an organic way, will create an organization that is greater than any individual element in that system, and greater than the sum of the elements in the system.

We can't directly understand complex systems, but we can model them and make some predictions based on those models. I have broken down organizational agility so that it can be understood with four key elements. Each of these elements holds one key to organizational agility and, just like human beings, won't survive without air, food, shelter and emotional connection. So, organizational agility will not exist without balance in the 4 Aspects of Agility.

The challenge in any organizational change is to keep all the pieces aligned as you move from the old to the new way. If any dimension is too far out of sync with the others, conflict and tension will be the result. This conflict and tension may serve to reinforce the move to agility or it may kill the change.

Our historical management/leadership, organizational culture, business systems and the technical ways we work have all been developed in and for contexts that no longer exist. Business in the early and mid-20th Century was focused on optimizing for assembly lines. If an organization is going to change to support the 21st Century business context, it needs to change and maintain balance in four key areas:

- Technical Practices

- Business Processes
- Organizational Culture
- Leadership Approach

You may have heard that agile is a mind-set or that agile is a culture change. When people say this, they are trying to shift the focus off of the items on the top half of the diagram (business processes and technical practices) and place the focus on the bottom items (organizational cultural and leadership approach). As discussed in Chapter 1, today's organizations are more engaged in knowledge work and thus require engagement and creativity more than compliance and conformance.

> *"We don't actually finish our films, we release them."*
>
> John Lasseter, Pixar

In the following sections we will explain what each of these areas is and some of the implications of each aspect. These are not intended to be a recipe for becoming agile, but a framework for understanding the balance in your organization.

The Technical Practices Aspect

Technical practices are the practical tools and techniques used by teams, management, and leadership to deliver products and services to customers. This is the kind of stuff you can learn in a workshop.

Traditional, sequential, 20th Century technical practices include:

- Assembly lines
- Batch and queue processing
- Time and motion studies
- Variance analysis
- Six Sigma

These technical practices worked on the assembly lines of the 20th Century. To a limited extent, they still work on the left side, the well-defined side, of the *Process Knowledge Spectrum.*

When moving to a more nimble organizational approach, you will be adopting agility enabling technical practices. Agility enabling technical practices do not merely make *exceptions* for the *possibility of change*, they are based upon the *certainty of change* and are designed to leverage change for the benefit of the customer and the business. Examples of agile enabling technical practices include:

- Pair development (pairing)
- Continuous integration
- Continuous delivery
- Retrospectives
- Loosely coupled modules
- Iterative and incremental delivery
- Refactoring

Some technical practices that are thought of as agile are actually part of what we are calling 21st Century management thinking. For example, pairing is a practice that helps reduce problems and broaden perspective. Every organization can benefit from pairing at multiple levels. I am on the board for the PMI Agile Community of Practice, and we pair in our leadership roles because we believe that having two heads is better than one, and that the throughput bottleneck of knowledge work is the thinking, not activity. So, having two people thinking is more productive than having just one. While this enables agility, it is also just good practice. Similarly, retrospectives are just good business practice and should be practiced by any organization.

On the other hand, iterative and incremental delivery is not necessary if you are operating in a context of well-known process knowledge, routine operations. Being iterative and incremental in the day-to-day operations of a fast food restaurant is not necessary or productive.

Technical practices are the easiest of the 4 Aspects of Agility to observe and evaluate because they are mostly observable. You can ask people if they hold a daily standup or if they are working iteratively, and observe to see if their actions match their words.

The Business Processes Aspect

Business processes are the continuously improving processes, procedures, tools, and policies that support the business. Agility enabling business processes enable managers and leadership to quickly assess a situation with just enough data to make critical decisions. They also support the prioritization of work that enables the delivery of customer and business value.

Agility enabling business processes support the technical practices and are reinforced by the organizational culture and leadership approach. They are the systems that enable teams, business leaders, analysts and managers to easily work together in tight knit groups to deliver customer value.

Examples of business processes include:

- Requirements management processes
- Planning and estimation processes
- Reporting processes
- Decision making models and processes
- Governance processes
- Budgeting processes
- Human Resources processes

All of these processes are impacted by a move to being more agile. Some to a greater degree than others. Let's take, for example, requirements management. Traditional requirements management systems include processes, procedures, templates and artifacts for creating a detailed specification document at the start of the work in order to clearly detail the entire scope of the work in an attempt to reduce risks and improve predictability. The scope of work is then turned into a work breakdown structure (WBS), network diagram and Gantt chart. Estimates are applied and a requirements tractability matrix is created to ensure that every requirement is delivered per the specification. The problem with all this is that the only constant in life is change, and the only way the requirements are not going to alter is if the sponsor goes into a coma as soon as the spec is completed.

New principles are applied to business systems to give them the ability to be nimble. Principles like:

- Simplicity – the art of maximizing the work not done
- Pull
- Emergent design
- Collective ownership
- Value prioritization
- Just in time

Let's look at requirements management designed with these principles in mind. If we want to be nimble, that means we want to be able to change as fast or faster than the changes that are happening in the business context in order to provide the customer with the most value and the best options. If we are going to do this, it makes sense to be able to pivot and do something new at any point. But we don't want to waste what we have done and throw away a bunch of work. So what do we do?

If we first prioritize all of our work so that it is delivering the most value to the customers as soon as possible, that is a good start. Then if we design the elements so they can be delivered in small loosely coupled pieces that are full, complete and really provide value by themselves, that is another good step.

Now I have a system that delivers the product in small increments prioritized by value. Awesome. But what about that big spec? Shouldn't we know the whole system up front? Well, not necessarily. What happens if things change? And things always change. What if we were to just put down reminders of the features we wanted? These reminders would have just enough information to jog our memories about what we were thinking. When we get closer, just before we are ready to build that part, we would have a discussion about the details. This way if something changes along the way that impacts the design or the architecture of the next feature, we haven't spent a lot of time designing it for the old way. Here is a great example.

I was working on a project for a company that had a core architecture component that would enable a lot of future flexibility. This core architecture component would enable future projects to just plug into this core system rather than interfacing with a bunch of other systems individually. Think of it like a bunch of interfaces all with unique requirements. When you have a new system come online you don't need to create unique interface to each of the other systems, you just create one interface to the hub. You can see how this would make life easier.

Unfortunately, the project that was attempting to implement this feature was going to run over schedule. It was a government regulated project that had penalties associated with it that would have resulted in a multi-million dollar fine. If it had been a traditional project, we would have designed the architecture of the whole system first. Then we would have done detailed design, and likely would have started to build when we realized that we were not going to make the schedule. Because this was a core architecture element, we would have had to completely re-architect the system. This would have cost us between 4-6 months. But because we had taken this kind of light weight approach to the business process of requirements specification, you won't believe what happened. We were able to execute the re-architecture in just *2 weeks*!

By applying agility enabling practices and 21st Century management thinking to business practices, you get a totally different approach to business systems.

The Organizational Culture Aspect

Your team will develop a culture. The question is, will it develop into a high performing amazing team or will it just get by or will it develop into a toxic team that people hate and leave as quickly as they can? I have been in all of these types of organizations. Maybe you have too. Teams form their culture, most often, by accident. The key to success is to make the team culture intentional. Create the best team environment possible so your people can do their very best work.

Culture is a set of organizational beliefs and behaviors. This set of organizational beliefs and behaviors define how people in the social structure behave. Culture is created and reinforced though the Cultural Reinforcement Model.

This model helps us understand how our everyday actions build a culture without our even realizing it. Think of each arrow as a bridge between the main island of memories to the islands of Thoughts, Beliefs, Actions, Results, then back to Memories. This series of paths is built of layers and layers of experience.   Every experience that follows the existing pattern reinforces the path.

 Let's walk through this cycle. When we come to a new social structure, we carry with us our previous cultural model. This new social structure either reinforces our model or challenges and, potentially modifies, our model.

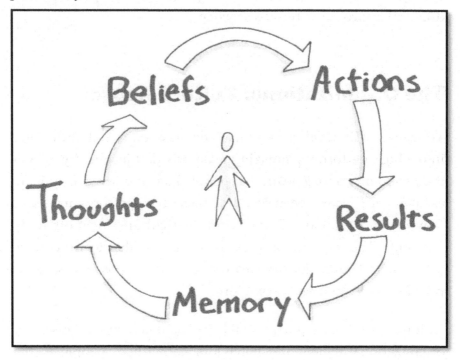

Imagine that you come to a situation that requires your action. What do you do?

- All your past results are stored in your memory.
- From that **memory** you draw thoughts of similar situations in your past.
- From your past experience you form **beliefs** that you should act one way or another.
- So, you take the **action**.
- This action has a **result**, either what you expected or not.
- This information gets stored as **memories** for future use.

If the results were as expected, your mind strengthens the path from that event to that result.

If the *result was different,* then it causes cognitive dissonance, stress in your brain because things don't match what you have experienced in the past. If it isn't a big deal, the dissonance will be minor and you may not even notice. But that memory goes into your brain.

Think of this new pathway in your mind as a pathway in the jungle that has only been walked on once. The old memories of previous results are a wide and well-worn path. But this new one is odd, an outlier. The next time you come to a similar situation you will most likely react the same way as you did before. The mountain of evidence for your action outweighs one little deviation from the pattern. Each time you get the new result, it makes the path a little wider, a little better defined, a little more attractive for the next time you have a similar experience.

At the same time, if those new layers are not being added to the old pathways, the old paths eventually lose their strength and the

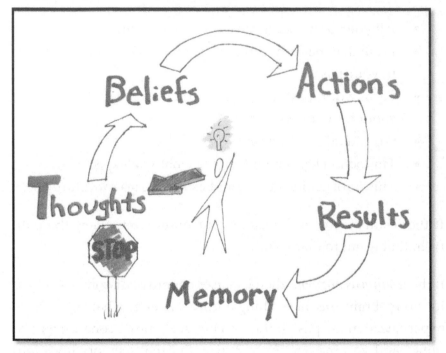

path becomes overgrown. At some point the new evidence outweighs the old and your default behavior will come from the new well-trodden path. This is the most common way new culture is established. Little consistent changes result in a new pattern being established. It is a long and slow process.

This is not the only way that culture is established. We can be intentional about culture. To intentionally change a culture we must create a new path, not by accident but by intention. We must override our memory with knowledge. Knowledge that creates a stronger belief than our experience can counter. This may be from listening to others we trust, from reading material, or from practicing exercises.

This is the metacognitive (thinking about thinking) approach to culture. It works more quickly than an organic approach, but it is much harder because you are intentionally going against your experience. The evidence that formed the belief must be very strong.

Every organization is different, so your journey will be different. But many organizations have a combination of 20th Century management thinking with command and control structures. To make a shift to being a 21st Century agile organization from this model will take significant cultural shifts.   The cultural shifts in an agile organization are moves to encourage agility from everyone.   This means our organizational response to situations will be different. One example is our response to failure.

Most organizational cultures see failure as bad. In an organizational culture where you are working iteratively though, failure can be good as long as it is coupled with learning and is a temporary stop on the way to greater success. Failure is just learning.

It is like skiing. If you ski, think about when you first learned. You fell a lot because you were learning.   Then, you got to a place where you could ski competently without falling all the time. Now you can ski and not fall. But if you do, you are playing it safe and aren't likely learning and improving.   If on the other hand you are falling all the time, you are probably going too far over your skills. There is a sweet spot where you are learning and improving, you are falling some and skiing more. Each fall teaches you more about skiing better.

It is the same way with agile new product development. Fall all the time and you are likely in the wrong market. If you never fall, then it is likely you are leaving business on the table. There is a sweet spot where you are making some mistakes and missteps, but mostly succeeding and selling.

Due to fear, many organizations build up processes and procedures to ensure that nothing goes wrong. Organizational fear is actually quite common; we just don't call it fear. Fear is the reason that we have so many projects in process at the same time. Fear is the reason that we over-regulate. Fear is the reason that we over-document. The list goes on...fear of failure, fear of being wrong, fear of losing business. The belief is that any perceived failure is worse than the cost of all that preparation. The unintended consequence of this build up is often lethargy, the opposite of agility.

The Leadership Approach Aspect

The leadership approach in 21st Century organizations is necessarily different from the leadership approach of Industrial Revolution organizations. As discussed earlier, during the Industrial Revolution the dominant approach to leadership was a command and control approach based in fear, fear of losing your job, fear of not getting a pay raise, or fear of public embarrassment. Because of the presence of these fear controls, leaders in these organizations can dictate how, when and where work will be done. Most established organizations use hierarchical organizational structures that inherently have a fear structure base in them. [7] For all the reasons above, we fear offending those *above* us in the hierarchy. This is not some kind of intentional attempt to scare people into compliance. At least not generally today. Although in the past, people at Ford could have been fired for smiling. The fear I am talking about is an undercurrent that is present but unacknowledged. Generally, we don't even know it is there.

The command and control approach was taken because it was easy, and it appeared to quickly convert the agrarian and crafts people of the time into model workers who would continually execute the same task over and over. Compliance was the desired outcome, not engagement or creativity. We know that knowledge work takes engagement and creativity.

In his book Drive: The Surprising Truth About What Motivates Us [8], Daniel Pink identifies three keys to motivation: autonomy, mastery and purpose. Having teams *self-organize* is important to enable agility and a 21st Century management thinking approach. However, allowing teams to self-organize is a cultural and leadership challenge. Self-organizing teams are autonomous and, when done right, people in these contexts are very motivated to work hard, succeed and achieve. I have a teenager and she really doesn't like being told what to do. But that's not surprising, who does? Everyone from children to adults like being autonomous.

We feel empowered. We feel strong when we are in control of our own destiny.

Too much autonomy

On the other hand, complete autonomy can be a scary. The complete lack of boundaries can actually create a different kind of fear - one that results when we don't know what to do or what is important. The fear generated from complete autonomy can be paralyzing. If you have kids, I am sure you can relate. When my girls are at other peoples' homes, I always hear how nice they are, so polite and how well mannered. But at home they are quite the opposite. They are not polite. They are not well mannered. They push back on us at every move. Have you ever wondered why that is? It is because at home they feel safe. They know us, they know the boundaries, and they know the rules. They know where the edges are and because they have tested those edges they are willing to push right up against them. Within the boundaries they are free to explore to the full extent. At other people's homes, they are not sure where the lines are drawn. They are unsure of the boundaries so they keep away from the edge. In creative work you don't want people to be afraid of the edges. You want them to push the boundaries. When fear takes over, we move from working in our cerebral cortex, where creative thought occurs, to our amygdala (lizard brain) where the only options are fight or flight. Creativity is pushed out when we operate in our amygdala. Leaders need to create a balance between too much freedom and not enough. [9]

Artists also set boundaries to help them be more creative. In dance, a choreographer may have a scene where they are working with a push broom, and every act has to be connected with the idea of sweeping. This boundary helps them get very creative and come up with ideas that they never would have considered without the limitation. Painting is the same way. Picasso's Blue period is the perfect example. By limiting himself to the color blue, he freed himself to be more creative than if he had the full pallet. [10]

Let no one fool you. When terms like self-organization are used, it is not in lieu of leadership. Leadership is necessary in any organization. Yet many leaders, when they first encounter self-organization, are concerned about self-organizing teams. We have spent so much time training leaders to control and direct work in the last century that it is very difficult to change the perspective. But that is just what is needed for knowledge work. Rather than directing the work, leaders in knowledge work context need to trust that they made good decisions in hiring and that these people are capable of self-organizing and doing the work. The leader's job is not to direct but to provide vision of what the teams should accomplish and set parameters around that vision, then do everything within their power to help the teams do their best work. This means that the primary job of the leader is to serve the team.

Chapter Summary

Whether you are attempting to change your team, department, division or entire company, you need to view your organizational move to 21st Century management thinking through the view of the 4 Aspects of Agility:

- Technical Practices
- Business Processes
- Organizational Culture
- Leadership Approach

Seeing your organization through the lens of the above practices will give you a more complete picture of what it takes to become agile and/or what might be slowing your move down. If it does not change with and support the technical practices and business processes, the gravity from culture and leadership will relentlessly pull the whole organization back to the way it was. All four aspects need to move, ideally in balance together. Just implementing new technical practices and/or business processes will not necessarily be a lasting solution.

Organizational culture and leadership should be aligned and supportive of the new way of working. This alignment may be just in your team or organizational unit, or it may be across the organization. When it does happen, the system will become not only self-sustaining but self-perpetuating and improving.

Selected Resources

http://searchcio.techtarget.com/tip/Four-ways-to-attain-business-agility

http://whitewaterprojects.com/2014/04/14/are-you-ready-for-business-agility/

Action Plan

Now What?

The four aspects of agility is a model for you to think about in your organization. Your challenge is to evaluate your organization in each of these areas and determine where your organization stands.

Think

Think about the 4 Aspects of Agility and consider your processes, procedures, culture and leadership. Are they exemplary of an agile organization?

Go to http://www.whitewaterprojects.com/4aspects/ to access our online resources to assess the 4 Aspects of Agility in your organization. Some of the resources are my own and some are links to other people's tools.

Think about your 4 Aspects of Agility and determine your greatest strength. Then determine to take some actions around that strength

Act

Now that you have determined your greatest strength, come up with a plan to do two things: 1) Determine how you can move that area to be even stronger; and 2) Determine how you can leverage the things that make this an area of strength into areas that you are naturally weaker. Use your strengths to lift your weaknesses.

Share

Share with your learning team your thinking; and together formulate more ideas for strengthening your strengths and leveraging those strengths into your weaknesses.

Some Core Practices

Six actions you can take today to move toward agility

Introduction

In this chapter we will briefly explore five items from the agile movement that project leaders can use on their work to improve effectiveness, visibility, create a positive culture, and increase the organization's overall agility. I have found these five items are things any organizational leader can do without much resistance from their team members or other parts of the organization. They are apparently innocuous enough.

It is important to remember when implementing any of these items that the whole picture of the organization must be considered. When an item only appears to deal with one aspect, consider the implications each item will have on the overall organization. Even the simplest practice can have complex and far reaching implications. Don't let this deter you from implementing these core practices today. Just be aware that your systems are more intertwined than you imagine.

Let's dive into these practices and see what you can do today to improve your work environment. The five items within the span of control for project leaders are:

1. Servant Leadership
2. Teamwork
3. Retrospectives
4. Value Stream Mapping
5. More Frequent Releases/Value Prioritization

I have purposely placed these items in this order for a purpose. While you could implement these in any order or implement them all at once, based on my experience I recommend this sequence. It isn't a hard and fast rule, just a suggestion. Throughout the chapter you will see how each item builds upon the previous items, and why I suggest this order.

This section is not intended to be an executive explanation of these core practices, but an introduction. There are whole books, classes and coaching on each topic. I will reference some books in each section for further exploration.

Ok, let's get started.

Servant Leadership

I start with servant leadership because it is completely within your control. You can do this without conferring with anyone and without getting anyone else to cooperate with you. Just start!

Servant leadership is an attitude of the heart, an attitude toward people. It is how you approach the role of leading. Servant leaders understand that they can do nothing on their own. They understand the most important thing to the success of their work is the people who are doing the work. Therefore, the most important thing they can do is help people. They do not abdicate their role as leader, but they approach it with humility and equality, even some self-deprecation.

This is not an artificial front, a façade, put on to manipulate. It is easy to make that mistake. Servant leadership is founded in integrity of character. The servant leader is genuinely concerned with the personal, professional, and spiritual growth and wellbeing of their team members and those around them.

The new 21st Century Leader is a *servant leader*. A servant leader focuses on serving the members of the team, organization, or community to help them be and do their very best.

Servant leadership is not a new idea; it has been around for just over 2000 years. Some of the greatest leaders of history were servant leaders:

- Jesus of Nazareth
- Abraham Lincoln
- Mahatma Gandhi
- Nelson Mandela
- Martin Luther King, Jr.
- Jimmy Carter
- Mother Theresa

They were all different in what they did. So, what do these people all have in common? The heart of all of them is their character. The one word we can use in common to describe all of them is *love*. Yes, love. It is a strange word, and one we don't use often enough in business. One of the problems is that English has only one word for love that is used in a multitude of ways: I love my wife, I love my brothers, I love my work, and I love my dog. All very different kinds of love. There is another kind of love. The kind that is completely selfless. The kind you see in firefighters who will risk their own lives to save someone else.

The kind of love I am talking about here is a selfless kind of caring for the other. A leader who is selfless, and always thinking of the best for the people they are serving, is the model of every leader listed above. The authority these people hold is not from a position of power, but from a position of love and respect.

When a leader takes the servant leader position, they do not tell their team what to do. They free their team to take ownership of the work. Yet, they provide boundaries within which the team can be free and creative.

The key to the success of self-organizing teams is equipping them with the information they need and *giving them the power* to make decisions locally. If every decision has to be made by one person or a small group of key decision makers, you will never scale. If, on the other hand, leadership really wants to get nimble, they will equip the team, trust them to do good work, and get out of the team's way. Things might not get done exactly the way the leader would have done them, but a lot more will get done.

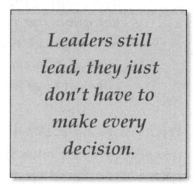

Leaders still lead, they just don't have to make every decision.

Equipping and trusting the team to make decisions does not mean the team is without direction. Leaders still lead, they just don't have to make every decision. The role of the leader is to set the *vision* and *parameters*. Great leaders have always lived this way. Martin Luther King, Jr. didn't tell the people of the Civil Rights Movement exactly how, when and where to protest. He set the vision and parameters. That's all. The *vision* was that the country would:

> *"... live out the true meaning of its creed: 'We hold these truths to be self-evident: that all men are created equal.'"* [11]

Martin Luther King, Jr. set *parameters*,

> *"We must forever conduct our struggle on the high plane of dignity and discipline. We must not allow our creative protest to degenerate into physical violence. Again and again we must rise to the majestic heights of meeting physical force with soul force."* [11]

With vision and parameters, MLK was able to align millions of people across the United States. The people had the vision and the parameters defining acceptable outcomes. Then, they were left to plan in their homes across the country. This is equipping and trusting; and it changed a nation!

When the leader takes the servant leader position, they free their team to take ownership of the work and that is a powerful shift. It takes a very secure leader to be a servant leader. Some leaders feel they need to be in control in order to feel important. A servant leader is confident enough to give the reigns over to others.

Servant leadership will change the way your group works. It will impact other leaders in your organization and your team. As with many of these practices, it starts in the Leadership Approach aspect of the 4 Aspects of Agility, but quickly moves to the Organizational Culture aspect. As you begin to serve your teammates, they will begin to serve each other. It may take some time but it will happen.

It is often helpful for a leader to enlist the aid of an external mentor or coach in making the shift from directive leader to servant leader because it can be difficult for us to see where we are being a servant and where we are not. Old habits die hard, and getting someone with fresh eyes can be very helpful. I also highly recommend taking a workshop and reading the work of James Hunter on servant leadership.

Teamwork

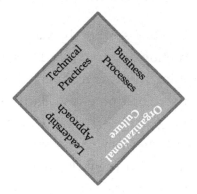

No single factor has more predictive power for the success or failure of your projects and programs than the health of your teams.

There are three elements that differentiate a team from a group of people:

- A sense of safety
- A goal for which we are mutually accountable
- Interdependence

Sports teams get this by design. Contrasted with individual sports, team sports have built-in mutual accountability for a goal, and interdependence. What doesn't come by design necessarily is safety.

My oldest daughter loves volleyball, just absolutely loves it. The girl sleeps with a volleyball tucked under her arm. No kidding! She has played for five years now and she is only 15. One year, she had a coach who had amazing skills. I couldn't believe that in the first couple of days this coach had them learning to "read" the body position of the opposing team to determine where the ball was going. In just a few minutes, he had the team calling out as a player was hitting where the ball was going to go. It was amazing!

Another season she had a different kind of coach. They were playing at a four day tournament. It was long and hard. To this point, the team had played well together but they weren't playing up to their potential. The coaches called a team meeting and had the girls do a team bonding exercise. (No parents were allowed and coaches were not permitted to speak. They were only there to facilitate.) The girls sat in a circle. One by one each girl was on the hot seat. The other girls would say one thing they appreciated about that girl. Every girl spoke. From the reports I heard, there were tears and joy. The coaches were astounded with what they heard. All of their beliefs and more were communicated by the girls on the team. It was a powerful and moving time.

What happened next is the proof of the power of psychological safety. They were playing a game at 9:30 PM after having played several other games that day. The team they were up against was one they had lost to in a previous meeting. Our girls played the best volleyball I had ever seen them play. The volleyball games are played to 25 points and the winning team has to win by 2 points.   In this game at 9:30 PM (late for a bunch of middle school girls who had played several games by this point), the opposing team had 24 points, we had 16. In most circumstances this would be a done deal. The other team would win. But not that night. Our girls fought back and won the game.

The coaches and parents were in awe. What had changed? They didn't get extra practice to play better, they didn't learn new techniques, and they didn't even spend time drilling. They just got to know each other, to care more for each other.   It made all the difference.

Great teams will only form when there is psychosocial safety. When we feel safe, we will trust; and trust is shown in our willingness to be vulnerable and take risks.

On June 30, 1859, Charles Blondon attempted the impossible, the unthinkable! He took to a thin wire stretched between the United States and Canada, over the boiling Niagara Falls and slowly walked the treacherous 1,100 feet. Watching from the U.S. side were 25,000 onlookers. Holding their breath with every step. Blondon proceeded to cross several more times, that day and over the following weeks. Each time raising the bar of danger. One time he crossed with a large camera (remember this was the 1800s), which he balanced on the wire, and took a picture of the audience. Another time he took a large cast iron stove with him and cooked an omelette which he lowered to the boat below the falls. On July 4th he crossed again. This time he took a wheelbarrow from one side to the next. People were amazed. At each crossing the uproar of applause was thunderous. Upon completion of his crossing, it is said, that the following exchange ensued:

> Blondon: "Was that crossing amazing?"
>
> Cheers from the crowd.
>
> Blondon: "Do you believe I can do it again?"
>
> "We do, we do!" shouted the crowd.
>
> Blondon: "Do you?"
>
> "Yes, yes, we do!" they cheered louder still.
>
> Blondon retorted, "Ok, then who will get in the wheelbarrow?"
>
> The once boisterous crowd now fell silent. No one volunteered. Time went by slowly, until one man stepped forward and got into the wheelbarrow. It was Blondon's manager and friend of many years. The two proceeded to cross the chasm together.

Whether or not that exchange really happened is a point of controversy; however, what is not debated is that on July 16th Charles Blondon did cross Niagra Falls carrying a person. He crossed with his manager holding onto his back. The details make little difference, in a wheelbarrow or on Blondon's back, it still shows great trust on the part of the passenger to put his very life in the hands of another. But note that the only person who took up the challenge was one who had a well-established sense of safety with Blondon.

You can say all day long that you trust someone, but until you are willing to put your success (in this case your life) into their hands,

trust is just a word. The same is true of vulnerability based trust. You can say all day long that you trust your teammates, but until you dare to take a risk and allow the possibility of failure, it is all just words.

The question then is how do you create psychosocial safety? A simple starting point is being deliberate about appreciation.

According to one Gallup Poll, 70% [12] of people are not engaged at work. Seventy percent! That is a lot. What makes people get engaged?

At least once a week, express what you appreciate about each team member, ideally in a public context. For example, in your next meeting when you hand off the next agenda item to your teammate, say, "Next we will hear from Susan about the budget. You know what I appreciate about Susan? She is always on time to our team meetings. Susan, the floor is yours." If you have never publicly appreciated your teammates, and many of us haven't, it might be awkward to begin with, but soon it will become second nature.

As a leader you will want to make sure people know you appreciate them. But it can be hard to know what everyone is doing. Actually, it is downright impossible to know what everyone is doing. So try this. Start by asking one of the team members privately, "Hey, tell me two people who have done something outstanding this week." When they give you the names and their accomplishments, go and find those people. Tell them what their co-worker said. "Hi, Susan, Mark told me what a great job you did with the Michelson account. I really appreciate that." Then ask them to identify two people who were outstanding and why. Very quickly you will have made the rounds to most everyone on the team. They will feel appreciated, and you won't have to come up with all the ideas yourself.

Creating a sense of safety, a connection to a common goal and deliberate interdependence in the work the team does will help you be a rock star team creator.

Retrospectives

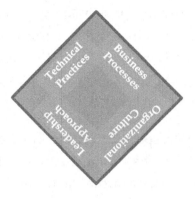

Retrospectives are a chance for the people on a team to reflect on how they are working and improve. In lean language this is known as kaizen: continuous small improvement to the system. The team meets frequently (every couple of weeks or every month at the least) to intentionally step back, not think about the work itself but to think about *how* they are doing the work. A retrospective impacts all four aspects of agility described in Chapter 5. The retrospective itself is a technical practice that often impacts business processes. You might even call it a business process as it is part of an overall business process for continual improvement. Holding retrospectives impacts culture by creating a context that validates learning from mistakes, being transparent, and working collectively to solve problems. It impacts leadership approach because the leaders either empower the team supporting them in the process of improvement, or the leaders' approach will shut it down and make the retrospective ineffective.

A lesson can only be said to have truly been learned when we act differently as a result. In traditional projects, lessons learned sessions are held at the end of the project. These sessions are intended to capture important lessons that can be used to improve the success of future projects. Unfortunately, these are largely, a waste of time. The lessons learned are either so general that they are useless, or they are so specific that they are useless to other projects. Finally, they happen after the project is done, the team has disbanded, and the project is implemented and no improvements can be made so the lesson cannot really be said to have been learned.

A retrospective, on the other hand, is a frequent, mid-project, version of a lessons learned. This shift is so simple and solves all the problems from the lessons learned. They are frequent, so the team can remember what they did a few weeks ago. You will still cover a lot of the same items:

- Project/context specific, *but the project is still going*!
- Technology/domain specific, and *you are still dealing with that technology/domain*!
- Team specific, and *the team is still together*!

Here is what makes the difference. At the end of the retrospective, the team determines what they are going to do about their top couple of items. They actually make a plan to address any issues. I always say, "A lesson isn't learned until you do something different." You can actually say you *learned* these lessons because the team takes specific action and solves the problems.

Next we will talk about the steps that make up a retrospective, but first I want to talk about what really will make or break the retrospective: facilitation. A well facilitated retrospective will be positive, interactive, and even fun. But a poorly facilitated retrospective will essentially be a gripe session. One retrospective closing activity I do is a simple exit sheet where people write down how the retro was for them. One former team member wrote the following comment:

> *This was the best experience I have ever had in a retrospective. My past experience had much more yelling and hurt feelings.*

Yelling and hurt feelings may result from poor facilitation. If the culture is particularly toxic, it is advisable to bring in an external person to facilitate the retrospective. This facilitator needs to be someone who is both kind and firm. They need to be able to create a sense of psychological safety in the session and be able to facilitate the difficult conversations that will inevitably come up. When handled well, retrospectives can be a great experience for everyone. The key is coming to the retrospective with the desire to learn. Norman Kirth's Retrospective Prime Directive is a great foundational agreement to have in a retrospective. The Prime Directive states:

> ***Regardless of what we discover, we understand and truly believe that everyone did the best job they could, given what they knew at the time, their skills and abilities, the resources available, and the situation at hand. [13]***

If everyone can at least start out with this mind-set, it will be helpful to everyone.

Retrospectives are very important; and facilitating brainstorming and knowledge sharing exercises can be challenging. Do your prep work, know what you are planning and expecting, and be ready to step in when things go sideways on you.

The typical retrospective has five steps:

1. Setting the Stage
2. Gathering Information
3. Generating Insights
4. Deciding What To Do
5. Closing the Retrospective

Setting the Stage - As we set the stage for a retrospective, we are defining for the team what we are trying to get out of the retrospective. We are checking in with each other to ensure everyone is present and not distracted by other things. We are setting the boundaries for the time we will be examining as we don't want to go all the way back to the beginning of time. Only the most current time frame will be reviewed.

Gathering Information – Now we gather information about the time period we are reviewing. What happened - good, bad or indifferent. What were the events, what were the problems and successes in the time period? We capture these in some form that we can use to evaluate and generate insights.

Generate Insights – Now that we have information, we need to examine the information, determine what relationships exist and what we want to address to find root causes. In this section we look at the good and the bad and their root causes. Typically, we have gathered enough information to pare down the list to the subset of most important issues, which can then be addressed.

Decide What To Do – Once we have determined root causes of the issues we have identified, we must decide what we are committed to do about them. This really sets retrospectives apart from a simple lessons learned. We actually decide what actions we are going to take, who is responsible for those actions and establish a target for getting it done.

Close The Retrospective – Finally, we close the retrospective. This can be as simple as saying thanks for coming and confirming the commitment of those who are taking action.

There are dozens of websites and books about retrospectives offering suggestions of exercises and techniques for each of the five steps. I suggest you check some of these out:

http://retrospectivewiki.org/

http://www.retrospectives.com/

http://www.plans-for-retrospectives.com/

Agile Retrospectives: Making Good Teams Great by Ester Derby and Diana Larsen. Pragmatic Bookshelf, 2006.

At my workshops, I challenge attendees to commit to going back to their offices and immediately scheduling a monthly recurring one or two hour retrospective. Virtually no one will stop you from this. The only argument I have heard is that people do not want to give up the time from their schedule. If you meet this objection, simply ask people to try it a couple of times. When retrospectives are well facilitated, people will ask for more!

Value Stream Mapping

Value stream mapping is a way of visualizing the flow of work through a system, identifying where the value-adding and non-value-adding work is done.

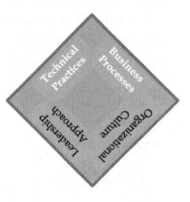

Value stream mapping is a technical practice and business process.

Once you have scheduled your retrospectives, I encourage you to map the value stream for your organization. You could do it before starting retrospectives, but having the retrospectives gives you a context to discuss the implications of what your team finds in creating the value stream map.

For many years I was involved in IT infrastructure construction projects at the Fred Hutchinson Cancer Research Center in Seattle,

Washington, USA. I was quite successful with the project I worked on. When I was assigned my first software project, I was excited because I was looking for new horizons to conquer. The project, however, was an abysmal failure.

We hired a contractor to rewrite some of the software. Well into the project I found that he seemed to be stalled. He kept giving me the "90% done" story. I was concerned at first, then worried. After a while I thought I would have a look at the code even though I hadn't written code since my Commodore64. I didn't want to embarrass him, or make it seem like I didn't trust him, so I waited until he had gone home. When I printed the code out I was astonished - first that I could understand it and second by how bad it was. Even I could tell what he was doing was not going to work, nor was it scalable. What should have been written in nested loops was written sequentially. It was awful. We ended up letting him go and getting someone else to do the work. We were late and over budget by this point.

One of the key things I learned from this experience is that progress is not naturally visible with knowledge work. With construction I could see the concrete being poured. I could see the core drills through the concrete and the PVC sleeves installed. I knew when the walls were being put in because…you could see the wall. Duh. With software, it isn't that way. Software and knowledge work involves an ephemeral substance, knowledge and the manipulation of information that is invisible. If you are going to be successful with managing knowledge work, you have to make it visible.

Value stream mapping is a process and a tool to make visible the invisible processes and flow of work in our organizations. The process is the discovery that it takes to create the map; and the tool is the map, once it has been created. On the surface it appears to only be a technical practice, and it can be, if it is hidden away. But the point of creating a value stream map is to visualize the work flow and, therefore, call attention to the trouble spots. This will have an impact on leadership and culture. Do not underestimate the importance of displaying the value stream map somewhere where people walking by will see it.

The value stream map will make trouble spots visible. If the surfacing of these trouble spots is not handled with a focus on support and problem solving, the people who work in those trouble spots may become defensive. As a leader in the organization, you need to recognize this and guide the culture - create moments to focus on the problem, not the person.

A value stream map shows the flow or lack of flow of any given product from the idea stage through delivery to customer and their feedback loop (if any). By mapping the value stream, we are focusing our energy on finding how our organization creates customer value and what adds value to our customers. By definition then, anything that is not adding value to our customers is waste and should be ruthlessly routed out of the system.

Mapping the whole value stream for an organization can be a very complex exercise. When you are just starting out, it is best to just start with your project or work flow.

Mapping the value stream in a system or organization is part of the lean process improvement approach. The diagram above shows the very generalized flow of any lean improvement project. The first step in the process is to identify value.

Value is defined by your customer. Ideally, you can ask them. Value is anything that is of worth or importance to a customer.

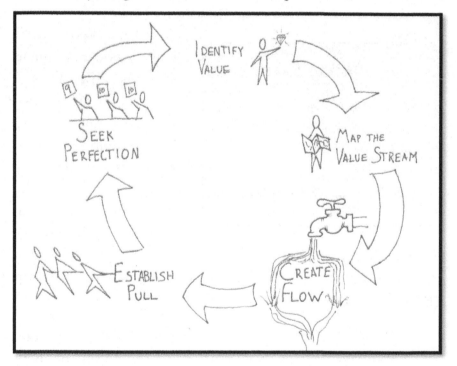

In most cases it can be identified by asking the question, "Would our customer pay for this?" That is the question I use most often. However, there are organizations that exist not for profit, but as a service organization. In these cases, it is still useful to ask the question but slightly modified, "If our constituents knew we were spending their money on this, would they approve?"

That is a good place to start. If you cannot determine what value is in your company, how do you know if your project is worth doing? Someone better be asking that question. This exercise alone has helped hundreds of organizations through lean transformation. Just determining what value means brings focus and clarity. Everything that doesn't add value is waste, and should be routed from your organization.

Online Extra

Watch this video for a quick tutorial on how to create a value stream map:

http://bit.ly/valuestreammap

Once you know what value is, you can begin to map its flow through your organization. I like to do this as a brainstorming session with my teams. It may be said that the brainstorming technique isn't as efficient as meeting with a couple of key people who best understand the process. However, I find there are a couple of benefits to the group approach:

1. The people who *know the system best* often don't really know the system. They know how it should run, not how it really runs.
2. It helps the whole team better understand the whole process and how they fit in the bigger picture.
3. Being part of the process creates a sense of buy-in.

The sociological benefits can't be emphasized enough. People need to have their opinions heard and they need to be validated.

Mapping the value stream can be as simple as identifying the steps in the process of the organization. Even if documentation exists outlining the processes in place, it is best to start from scratch. What we want to see is the real flow of value, not the idealized business process. The real business process is much messier than what we idealize in business process documentation.

Don't use a computer to map the value stream. The best way is to just use paper and pencil, or if you are in a conference room, use a whiteboard. Using paper and pencil (not pen) helps people understand that this is all draft. Once something gets typed up on a computer, there is some kind of feeling that it is official. This isn't an overt thing we do, it is somewhere deep in our psychology.

This brainstorming session is just a first pass, but it will provide a high level view. There are always hidden steps in nearly any process (some approval that so and so needs to provide, or a review by the *xyz* committee) that isn't part of the formal process but happens all the time. These hidden processes are what you want to find and the ones that the team will be able to tell you about, typically better than department heads or executives.

Next, lay out the process steps on a whiteboard or other big visible chart on the wall. Again, don't do it in a computer. The point of having the chart is so people see it. If the value stream map exists in a computer somewhere, people will have to go find it. That isn't as powerful as a big map on the wall that people see every time they walk by it.

Under each process step put two columns: "Doing" and "Done". Each column should be wide and tall enough to fit sticky notes.

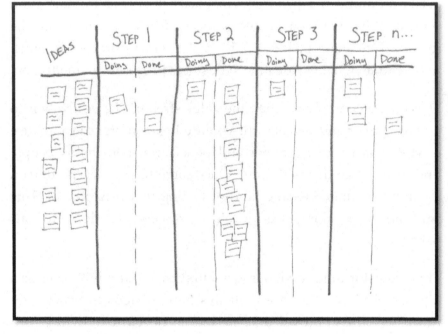

The next task is to create those sticky notes - one for each piece of customer value that is flowing through the system. Ideally, you will have one flow for all of the work your team members have to work on. One chart that shows all of their work. That way you can easily see what people are working on.

Use this chart to visualize the invisible workflow in your organization. So much of what we do is invisible. Making it visible allows us to see where potential and actual problems lie.

You will find over time one or more of the columns becomes clogged with work. This is your bottleneck. But that isn't a problem, every system has bottlenecks. They have to have bottlenecks or there would be infinite flow in the system. Your goal is not to eliminate bottlenecks, but to use them to optimize the system. If this is a stretch for you to conceptualize, read "The Goal" by Eli Goldradtt.

There are numerous ways we can use this chart to optimize and improve your organization, but a detailed discussion of those things would be a book in itself. Just having the chart and visualizing your work will help your organization begin to see where problems lie, allowing you to address them.

When you are acting in the model of a servant leader, your teams will feel safe. They will know you are not going to use the value stream map to beat them up. Having the work visualized will help your organization see the invisible, give attention to the trouble spots, and address them in your team retrospectives. Are you starting to figure out how these things fit together?

Frequent Releases
Value Prioritization

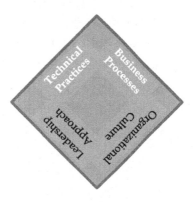

The last practice you can and should introduce is frequent releases of value prioritized functionality. This impacts business processes because you have to decide how to break down the work in a new way. You have to learn to break it down very small and prioritize the work that in the past was just called *scope*. Increasing the number and frequency of releases impacts technical processes because the team has to figure out how to technically implement the work in more phases.

In the traditional projects I used to do, we would always have a scope of work that was required for the project. When all of the items were complete, the project was done. If the project was done on time and under budget, it was a success. If it was late or over budget, it was a failure. On a rare project, we would have features categorized in three groups: Must have, Could have, Would like to have...or something like that. But in practice, these were never really used to manage scope as the whole scope was expected.

In reality, some features are more important than others, some are used more, some are not even necessary. Additionally, some parts of some features are not necessary but because they are rolled up in the larger feature they have to be done.

In adding more releases, you are going to ask your project leaders to prioritize every feature in the system. Every feature! Not just into groups, but in a sequence of priority based on value to the customer. Ideally, they will break down the work to a fine granularity as well so that individual aspects of the features can be prioritized. But even if you just get them to prioritize the work in the chunks they conceive of the work, it will be a win.

Breaking the work down to greater granularity will be one of the most important ways we can improve our velocity of delivery. But in some organizations, this is too much to ask the first time out.

Think about it. If a feature X consists of items A, B and C, and in this scenario feature B is really the most important one, the product could be released to customers with just feature B. Let's also assume item A takes three weeks, B takes two weeks and C takes four weeks. Under

Online Extra

Watch a powerful video on the Business Value of Agile

http://bit.ly/leanagilevalue

our traditional, deliver it all, approach, our customers have to wait nine weeks to use our product! If we break it apart though, they only have to wait two. When you do the math on the ROI Impact, it is quite amazing. Watch the online extra for an overview of the business value impacts of value prioritized releasing.

The next item is to deliver more frequently. I am not talking about releasing every two weeks or anything. Just look at your projects and see if you can double the number of releases. Contrary to the agilest claim, most of our traditional sequentially managed projects don't deliver in a big bang. We typically deliver in a couple of releases or phases. All I want you to do is to increase the frequency of those releases. If you have two releases, then have four. If you have four releases, ask for eight releases.

If you have prioritized the work and are releasing it in priority order, you will find that the last release is a bunch of low value, add-on items for features currently being used. When you get there, and not before, point out to your portfolio management or project sponsors that the team is now working low priority and the next project in line will deliver a lot more value to their customers. Trying to get people to cut these feature add-ons earlier would have been nearly impossible. But when faced with real choices like this, the decisions make themselves quite obvious.

Chapter Summary

In this chapter we have reviewed five key practices any project leader can use to begin to improve their delivery and culture. It is important to know that while each of these practices centers in one of the four aspects of agility, they all have implications in each aspect. For example, more frequent releases/value prioritization appears to be a combination of a technical practice (breaking down the work into more releases) and business process (prioritizing the work), but it has even more important implications for leadership and culture. The project leadership will be required to prioritize the work, something they are not used to doing as they are used to things being either in scope or out of scope. Additionally, the organizational culture is not designed to stop a project before the scope is complete. Stopping a project before all of the work is done will take culture change because it may appear to be a "project failure" when it really is the best kind of success.

These five practices: Servant Leadership, Teamwork, Retrospectives, Value Stream Mapping and Frequent Releases are the easiest to begin to use and can change the way you do work on a day to day basis.

Appendices

The Agile Manifesto

A bit of history and context

In February of 2001 a group of 17 software development consultants (and one methodologist from the DSDM Consortium) gathered together in Snowbird, Utah at what was billed as, "The Lightweight Methods Workshop." They came to talk about what they were finding as they were trying to develop software with lighter weight management and more flexible planning than traditional methods. They wanted to talk with peers and see what kind of commonalities there were. There were many. And the group had great conversations. Or so I am told. I have interviewed several of the attendees of the conference. Project managers at this time were attempting to apply methods and practices of other

On-Line Extra

Hear Ward Cunningham share what it was like at Snowbird that year at:

http://bit.ly/ward_interview

disciplines like construction to software development. Construction project management was being applied assuming that theoretically, it should work. The problem was that software is different from construction. One big difference is in the fact that software can be developed modularly with much fewer dependencies than necessary in construction.

The authors of the Manifesto had not really intended to create anything. They just wanted to share what they were doing and find some support in like-minded individuals. At one point the conversation came about that they were not against the items that they listed on the right side of the Manifesto but that they wanted less of them. It took less than 45 minutes for the group to write the four statements comprising the Agile Manifesto for Software Development. They came very quickly. After the fourth item they asked, "What would be the fifth item?" They couldn't come up with a fifth so they left it as it was. It was surprising to them.

Up to this point, the term "agile" had not been used to describe what they were doing. No one liked the term "lightweight" as it implied being wimpy. None of the attendees I spoke with could recall exactly who used the word "agile," but at some point through conversation they all agreed it conveyed the right idea.

The one negative was that they were all aware of Agile Construction. While they didn't want to be associated with other engineering approaches, the term seemed to fit best, so it stuck.

The Agile Manifesto has been a great rallying point for the various approaches to come around. It helps to both identify with each other as a community and to differentiate the agile movement from traditional approaches. Much of the growth of the agile movement can be attributed to the simplicity and universal nature of the Manifesto.

To many people, the Agile Manifesto is the definition of what it means to be agile. Not to me. If you take some time and look at the history of the Agile Manifesto, you will find that it was written by a group of men who were all doing similar things in their attempts to develop software in their various companies. As they did, they found there were actually remarkably similar threads that allowed them to quickly develop software and adapt to the changing whims of the dot-com industry which was so hot at the time.

Notice that what drew them together was the commonality of their successes in being agile. They were looking for common themes that helped them be agile. They were not trying to define agile. They were trying to define those things that were useful to them in successfully delivering software. Defining these commonalities in approach allowed them to talk with a common language about the differences between old style "command and control" and sequential approaches, and the new lighter weight approaches in which they were seeing success.

The definition of the Agile Manifesto was an important turning point in the spread of these approaches that enable an

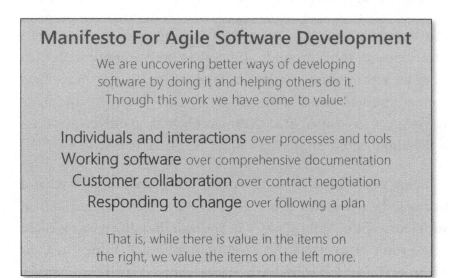

organization to be agile. Many other organizations have influenced the Agile Movement to a greater or lesser degree. Organizations such as the Agile Alliance, Scrum Alliance, ICAgile, Scrum.org, Agile Leadership Network, and others. All of the above organizations and the vendors, the articles, blogs and websites, and more constitute the "Agile Movement" - a general movement that promotes and encourages adoption of agility and agility enabling practices.

Myths

Some things people believe about agility that are just not true.

Introduction

With every controversial new topic or movement, there are truths and myths intermingled. So it is with agility. There are a number of myths about the common approaches to being nimble that seem to be quite persistent. Let's address these directly and be done with them. The most common myths are:

- "We don't do planning in agile."
- "Agile is just undisciplined cowboys."
- "Agile might work for small projects but not for large ones."
- "Agile is only for software."
- "Agile is Scrum."
- "You cannot have fixed requirements in agile."
- "We are agile; we don't do documentation."
- "We cannot use agile on this project, it is too high risk."

- "If we would just do agile, it would solve our {x} problem."

No planning

This myth, as do a couple other myths, stems from a misunderstanding of the Agile Manifesto. The source of this myth is found in the statement:

We value responding to change

Over following a plan

It is easy to see how one could interpret this statement to believe that there is no planning. Especially if they have been abused by schedule hounding project managers for decades. Ward Cunningham said, "You know we aren't really against these things we want to do less of, we just want to do less of them." The problem stems from not reading the whole manifesto. The last line in the Manifesto reads:

> *That is while there is value in the items on the right, we value the items on the left more.*

The writers of the Manifesto were not saying they hated documentation or that it should be eliminated, they were conveying it should be deemphasized. For years they had been forced to use the traditional sequential approach to project management and were not seeing a whole lot of benefit for the amount of oppression that came with it. Yes, *oppression* is a strong word. I have spoken with many developers who feel that strongly about this oppression, so I want to honor their feelings.

This myth is actually the opposite of what is true. Truth be told, there is actually more planning in organizations that are agile. The difference is that in traditional/sequential projects the planning is all done upfront by a small group of people, usually subject matter or technical experts and project managers. This plan is supposed to be managed and updated along the way.

Nimble organizations opt for *just in time* planning. Creating just enough structure to get moving and have a direction, but not trying to pretend more can be known that is possible. Events in the future are left intentionally vague and elaborated only when they come closer into view.

Traditional planning for a two year project may take weeks or months. Creating an agile plan can be done in a matter of hours with the knowledge it will be refined and tuned as we go. Items that are close in time are elaborated in more detail, while items further out are left more ambiguous.

Planning for change is not the same as creating a plan to control change. The most common approach to planning in agile organizations is a five layer model which includes:

1. A Vision – Very High Level (Fits on ½ Page)
2. A Roadmap Plan – High Level Themes and Ideas
3. A Release Plan – Specific Planned Dates by Quarter
4. An Iteration Plan – Detailed Plan for the Current Work in Process
5. A Daily Plan – Daily Coordination amongst Team Members

This kind of planning is done quickly and kept as high level/ detail-less as possible and reasonable for the work. This allows nimble organizations to respond to changes quickly and adapt the planning without a lot of lost work or creating a lot of new work. Several values from Lean Manufacturing and the Agile Manifesto for Software Development are played out in this type of planning:

- Responding to change over following a plan.
- Welcome changing requirements, even late in development. Agile processes harness changes for the customer's competitive advantage.
- Working software is the primary measure of progress.
- Simplicity - - the art of maximizing the work not done - - is essential.
- Remove the waste of over-processing (over-planning)
- Just In Time (JIT)

Like development, planning is done iteratively and incrementally over time and by the appropriate people at the time. Iteration planning is done at the start of each iteration, not before. This discipline allows changes to be made to the detail of the iteration up to the last reasonable minute (Just In Time) without having to throw out a lot of work. Unlike traditional sequential projects that attempt to know everything at the start of a project.

Each of the five phases of planning in a lean/agile system drills down to the next level of detail at the appropriate time. As you can see from the following diagram, each phase requires a little more detail and a little more planning.

No discipline

I believe this myth is just another manifestation of the fear of no planning. But it also stems from the exceptionally badly named approach called XP or Extreme Programming. Dubbed thus in the 1990s when everything was about being extreme: extreme sports, extreme soda, extreme ironing...Well along came Extreme Programming. It was defined as *extreme* because it stripped away everything not necessary for actually creating working software and called for things like pair programming and self-organizing teams. XP called for the elimination of documentation, except for that which was necessary. Saying that does not mean there would be no documentation, but "no documentation" is how it was taken by some who didn't really understand.

In some cases, XP was development without discipline. Cowboy coders just running amuck and calling it XP. But let there be no doubt, XP is highly disciplined. Those cowboy coders were not practicing XP. They were using XP as an excuse.

Again, a misinterpretation of the Agile Manifesto for Software Development contributes to the confusion here. When some people read the Agile Manifesto, they think it says there is no planning, no documentation, no management, no discipline; but it is not saying that at all. Just like the "No Planning" myth, this myth is a failure to understand and a failure to read the actual Manifesto.

Let's look at the lean and Agile Manifesto principles that address the lack of discipline question:

- Continuous attention to technical excellence and good design enhances agility.
- Build projects around motivated individuals. Give them the environment and support they need, and trust them to get the job done.
- The best architectures, requirements, and designs emerge from self-organizing teams.

In practice, agile approaches require *more discipline* than traditional sequential approaches, not less. This discipline is especially focused on the people in the field, the men and women in the trenches, on the line, the ones doing the work. In the traditional sequential approach, a group of knowledgeable project managers, subject matter experts and lead developers create a plan. Then, the project manager and a manager or two assign people to the tasks. Each person need only know what their boss told them to do in order to work on the project.

> In practice, agile approaches require *more discipline* than traditional sequential approaches, not less.

The best agile enabling practices allow the team to decide and create its own plan. Because no one is handing a plan down and directing the work, teams are designed to be self-organizing and, therefore, self-disciplined. There isn't a manager telling you what is important. You, the worker, have to know and understand the big picture, and be able to figure out what is most important to work on in the moment. Yes, the big picture is developed by management, but they are not directing the implementation. Work is brought to highly performing teams who should be trusted.

Only for small projects

The notion that agile is only for small projects is a very interesting myth because most of my work has been on large projects with hundreds of people on them. So, the students in my classes hear that perspective. I don't hear this myth very often from my

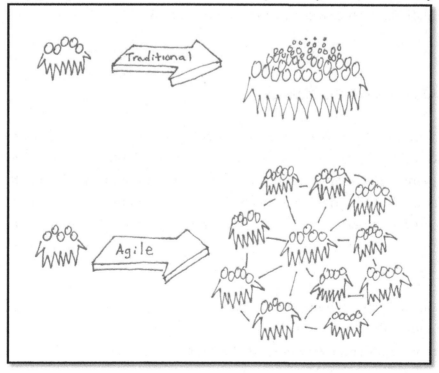

students. Actually, I have heard the opposite from clients I have worked with over long periods. They wonder if you can use an agile approach with small projects.   Funny, isn't it?!

The answer is "Yes!" You can run large and small projects with methods allowing agility.   Each project will look different. Think of it this way. Scaling traditional/sequential projects from small to large is like taking a small balloon and blowing it up really big. But scaling agile is like blowing up a bunch of little balloons. See the illustration. One key aspect of creating a nimble organization is communication. Communication doesn't scale beyond about nine people. Thus, if you want to scale, you don't scale the team size, you scale the number of teams. These teams then need a scaffold of other cross team communication.

Only for software

Yes, the Agile Manifesto was written by a group of software developers. And, yes, software development lends itself nicely to being agile because of the ability to work in nonlinear ways with code. But that does not mean that only software can be agile.   I think it is pretty obvious by our definition that all companies in the 21st Century need to be nimble as their business context requires.

But to really debunk the "software only" myth, I need only direct you to the document that first used the word Scrum to describe new product development that is agile:

"Under the rugby approach, the product development process emerges from the constant interaction of a hand-picked, multidisciplinary team whose members work together from start to finish. Rather than moving in defined, highly structured stages, the process is born out of the team members' interplay... A group of engineers, for example, may start to design the product (phase three) before all the results of the feasibility tests (phase two) are in. Or the team may be forced to reconsider a decision as a result of later information. The team does not stop then, but engages in iterative experimentation. This goes on in even the latest phases of the development process." [14]

This article, from the Harvard Business Review in 1986, was about the development of hardware, not software.

Much of the misconception is because people equate Scrum or XP with agility. It is true that both Scrum and XP were developed for software development. But the values and principles they were created from extend back to Toyota, lean manufacturing and lean product development, all of which are not software based.

As you see from reading this book, agility is critical in nearly all businesses these days, not just for software. Applying the principles found in this book will take critical thinking; it is not as easy as implementing a pre-packaged methodology. Your business is not like any other business out there, so why would your processes mirror someone else's processes?

Agile is Scrum

Scrum is great. It is a framework that enables agility and is easy for software development teams to implement. It can result in quick gains in productivity and huge gains in the ability to adapt to changing requirements. When implemented well, it can allow the creation of a wonderful working environment. That said, it is but one way to become agile, and it might not work in your context if:

- Your organization is not ready to dedicate people

- You cannot create stable, cross functional teams

- You cannot dedicate a Product Owner

Without these three elements, you cannot effectively use the Scrum framework. That is not to say you should not implement the Scrum framework. The framework was not created to fix all of your problems, but to make them visible. Hopefully, you can get at least two of the items above. Then, you will be able to make the third one very visible. If you are only able to get one of the items above, it will be very hard to use Scrum. And if you cannot get any of the items above, it will be nearly impossible. Not impossible, but very, very hard. Your focus will need to be on resolving one of the above three obstacles at a time.

Can't have fixed requirements

Ok, this myth is a little more delicate. Fixed requirements are quite a problem. But more often than not, requirements are not fixed. I know you will try to tell me that there are some projects where they are; for example, federally regulated projects have fixed requirements. I have worked on federally regulated projects and what I found is that they have a *fixed outcome*, they do not define what you do or how you achieve those outcomes. Thus the requirement is not fixed as much as the outcome.

Another tact to take when faced with seemingly fixed requirements is to break them down, way down. Traditional projects have a fixed set of requirements set in the project scope documentation, or maybe in a requirements specification. What we discussed in the Core Practices chapter is that these requirements should be prioritized and executed in that order. What I often find is that breaking down the requirements specification helps us see that not everything is actually necessary. If you break the individual features down further, there are often aspects, settings, and attributes that are less important and some that are more. Thus in breaking down these elements, we find even more that can be prioritized. The more granularly we can breakdown and prioritize the elements, the more quickly we can implement the minimum set of important elements, decreasing the risk to the project.

That said, if you did have a project that has fixed requirements for some reason, I believe you should still use the methods found in this book because they will improve your ability to deliver, to see clearly how the work is flowing, where you are in the process, and reduce risk.

No documentation

This one stems from a couple of misconceptions, one being the statement in the Agile Manifesto:

We value working software

> *Over comprehensive documentation.*

The problem arises when you don't read the whole Manifesto. The last line in the manifesto is this:
That is while there is value in the items on the right, we value the items on the left more.

The writers were not saying they hated documentation or that it should be eliminated, just that it should be deemphasized.

This issue is most prominently seen in the software industry so I will use examples from software in this section. Interestingly, other industries that are becoming agile don't seem to have this misconception as often.

There is still the very real need for documentation. Some regulated projects require documentation. End users may need reference material. However, if the software is well written and tested, users should be intuitive enough that documentation is not necessary. This is the expectation of most users today.

Another misconception is the idea from eXtreme Programming that *the code is the documentation*. This is sometimes taken to mean that developers must write a bunch of documentation into the code, or it is taken that because we wrote some code we don't need documentation. This is close but not quite on the mark. What is meant is that cleanly written high quality code should be readable by anyone and thus becomes documentation of the code. Yes, developers should write some comments in the code to help clarify but not to be supplemental documentation. Code should be clean and clear. If it is not, then it increases risk on future efforts to improve or extend the code.

Tests also provide a source of documentation. Well written unit and feature level tests will provide a clear logical map of the software and how it works. This is another reason to do test driven development.

So what if you do need documentation? When I have worked on efforts that required documentation, typically regulated systems that need auditing, I have the team put the required documentation in the team's *definition of done (DOD)*. The definition of done is the measure that the team uses to determine if a feature is complete and ready to demonstrate to stakeholders or ready for production. Let's assume you are using Scrum. By making it part of the DOD, you will ensure the documentation is completed with the feature. Some people like to put documentation in the backlog as a story. The problem with this approach is the story can get deprioritized in the backlog. They may be picked in the sprint with the feature but might not get done, if the feature is completed but the documentation is not, the documentation will slip to the next sprint, and then it is very likely that it will be deprioritized. You can see all the problems that come when documentation is held as separate from the DOD.

We can't use agile, this project is too high risk

If this myth wasn't so serious, it would make me laugh. The best practices used to become agile are generally there to reduce or mitigate risks. The truth is, you need to take an agile approach *precisely because the project is high risk.*

The following are the biggest risks on any project:

- Deliver nothing
- Deliver the wrong thing
- Deliver the right thing too late
- Deliver something that does not work

Taking an agile approach immediately mitigates these risks. We demo small increments to ensure we are delivering what the customer wants. We deliver the most important features upfront and the less important features later so we know we will be able to deliver on time. We deliver working products and usable services incrementally so we know all along that what we deliver will work. There is no last minute guessing, hoping, and praying that it will work.

Surprises are not what you want when risk is high. On high risk projects you need transparency so that you and everyone else know what is going on in the project.

Risk is addressed throughout the lifecycle of an agile effort and especially defined at three key intersections: initial planning, delivery planning and daily planning.

In initial planning we identify internal and external risks to the project. We identify high level feature risks so they may be tracked and incorporated into planning. Lastly, we identify and track schedule risks. These risks are all updated in the next two intersections.

At delivery planning intersections, either iterations or releases, we review and update the risks on individual features. Because we are drilling down more at this point on the details of the feature, we will also uncover more risks, which are added to the risk tracking and managed. A common approach for tracking risks is a risk burndown chart. This is a simple visual depiction of the risks associated with the release. They are often depicted in days of delay but may be shown as a financial risk factor. Each risk is evaluated for impact and probability and given a numerical value. These values are charted and updated on a periodic (typically weekly) basis. As we get closer to the risk trigger events and/or as we respond to the risk, we will know more about the risk and the value may go up or down. Once we pass the risk trigger, the risk is removed from the risk burndown.

Finally, on a daily basis we ask the question, "Are there any roadblocks?" This is a risk question. We are essentially asking if any risks have been realized or if there are any new ones. New risks are added to the risk burndown chart.

So as you can see, agile is actually designed for high risk efforts and nearly every aspect of becoming agile is there to address risk.

Agile will fix our problems

Finally, one of the most pervasive and least understood myths – *agile will fix our problems*. People often hear about the great things that others are doing when they are using an agile approach. They believe that because other people are seeing success, their problems will also be solved if they use the same methods and tools. Unfortunately, what they do not see is that the success is hard-won through struggle and adversity. Becoming agile won't solve your problems, but it will make them visible and quite often it will intensify your problems and force you to address them. Lean is the same way. The goal in lean is perfection, but no one thinks they can reach it. But the goal is to continually push toward it. This is the *Kaizen* mind-set, small iterative and incremental movements toward perfection.

When you start your journey to become agile, you need to understand that you are beginning a journey without an end. There are a number of models for organizational change. But most of them are linear. John Kotter's eight step process is a great example. His model starts with creating a sense of urgency, and ends with institutionalizing the change. What we are creating, however, is an organization that is in a constant state of re-examination and change. It is cyclical, not linear. In this model, change is the constant and people are the central and all important element.

Works Cited

[1]   Sentis, "Neuroplasticity, By Sentis," Sentis, 6 11 2012.
[Online]. Available:
https://www.youtube.com/watch?v=ELpfYCZa87g.
[Accessed 10 10 2014].

[2]   D. M. Maino, "Neuroplasticity: Teaching an Old Brain
New Tricks," Review Of Optometry , 1 1 2009. [Online].
Available:
http://www.revoptom.com/continuing_education/tabv
iewtest/lessonid/106025/dnnprintmode/true/skinsrc/.
[Accessed 10 10 2014].

[3]   D. Fisher, "Effective Use of of the Gradual Release of
Responsability Model," Learning Tree, 12 2008. [Online].
Available:
https://www.mheonline.com/_treasures/pdf/douglas_
fisher.pdf. [Accessed 29 8 2014].

[4]   J. Kotter, Leading Change, Harvard Business Review
Press, 2012.

[5]   theFreeDictionary.com, "The Free Dictionary," Farlex, 10
        10 2014. [Online]. Available:
        http://www.thefreedictionary.com/AGILE. [Accessed
        10 10 2014].

[6]   K. Beck, M. Beedle, A. van Bennekum, A. Cockburn, W.
        Cunningham, M. Fowler, J. Grenning, J. Highsmith, A.
        Hunt, R. Jeffries, J. Kern, B. Marick, B. Martin, S. Mellor,
        K. Schwaber, J. Sutherland and D. Thomas, "The Agile
        Manifesto for Software Development," 13 2 2001.
        [Online]. Available: http://agilemanifesto.org/.
        [Accessed 10 10 2014].

[7]   A. Edmonson, "Working Knowledge," 20 3 2006.
        [Online]. Available:
        http://hbswk.hbs.edu/item/5261.html. [Accessed 10 10
        2014].

[8]   D. Pink, Drive: The Surprising Truth About What
        Motivates Us, Riverhead Books, 2011.

[9]   J. Nelson, Positive Discipline, New York: Random House,
        Publishing Group, 2006.

[10]   J. Cameron, The Artist's Way, London, England:
        Souvenir Press Limited, 1998.

[11]   M. L. King, "Martin Luther King, Jr.," 28 8 1963. [Online].
        Available:
        http://www.archives.gov/press/exhibits/dream-
        speech.pdf. [Accessed 10 10 2014].

[12]   Gallup, "The State of the American Workpalce," 11 6
        2013. [Online]. Available:
        http://thegallupblog.gallup.com/2013/06/gallup-
        releases-new-findings-on-state.html. [Accessed 10 10
        2014].

[13]   N. Kirth, "Retrospectives Prime Directive," Norman
        Kirth, 4 10 2014. [Online]. Available:
        http://www.retrospectives.com/pages/retroPrimeDirec
        tive.html. [Accessed 10 10 2014].

[14]   I. Nonaka and H. Takeuchi, "The New New Product
        Development Game," *Harvard Business Review*, pp. 137-
        146, 1986.

[15]   R. Sheridan, Joy, Inc., Portfolio Hardcover (Penguin),
        2014.

[16]   W. a. R. Z. Samuelson, "Harvard Kenedy School," 1988.
        [Online]. Available:
        http://www.hks.harvard.edu/fs/rzeckhau/SQBDM.pdf

[17]   T. Roberts, Ed., Online Collaborative Learning: Theory and Practice, Ideal Group Inc, 2004.

[18]   C. Pellerin, How NASA Builds Teams, New York: WIley, 2009.

[19]   P. Lencioni, The Five Dysfunctions of a Team, Jossey-Bass, 2002.

[20]   D. H. H. Jason Fried, Remote: Office Not Required, Crown Business, 2013.

[21]   C. H. a. D. Heath, The Switch; how to change when change is hard, Crown Books, 2010.

[22]   A. Edmonson, Teaming: How Organizations Learn, Innovate, and Compete in the Knowledge Economy, Jossey-Bass, 2012.

[23]   R. DuFour, "https://www.youtube.com/watch?v=0hV65KIItlE," 9 October 2009. [Online]. [Accessed 20 8 2014].

[24]   E. Catmull, Creativity, Inc., Random House , 2014.

[25]   K. Blanchard,
         "http://www.kenblanchard.com/img/pub/pdf_critical
         _role_teams.pdf," 13 January 2009. [Online]. [Accessed 19
         8 2014].

[26]   Sinek, Simon, "Why Leaders Eat Last," 4 December 2013.
         [Online]. [Accessed 19 8 2014].

[27]   Martin Luther King, "United States National Archives,"
         28 August 1963. [Online]. Available:
         http://www.archives.gov/press/exhibits/dream-
         speech.pdf. [Accessed 10 10 2014].

Index